Elmer Wyse

FREEDOM isn't FREE

A BOAT PEOPLE STORY
Evelyn Friesen
as told by Phu Sam

Kindred Press

Winnipeg, MB, Canada   Hillsboro, KS, U.S.A.

Freedom Isn't Free

Copyright © 1985 by Board of Christian Literature,
General Conference of Mennonite Brethren Churches.

All rights reserved. With the exception of brief excerpts for reviews, no part of this book may be reproduced without the written permission of the publisher.

Published simultaneously by Kindred Press, Winnipeg, Manitoba, R2L 2E5 and Kindred Press, Hillsboro, Kansas, 67063.

Cover Design by Kathy Penner, Winnipeg.

Printed in Canada by The Christian Press, Winnipeg.

International Standard Book Number: 0-919797-47-4

To my father, Jake Friesen, for his dedication and involvement in sponsoring Vietnamese refugees and his encouragement in compiling this book.

INTRODUCTION

When the tragedy of the thousands of southeast Asians fleeing Vietnam by boat burst upon the consciousness of the world, the Canadian government organized a private sponsorship program. Churches and small groups of individuals across the country undertook full responsibility for one year for the well-being of the refugees that they agreed to sponsor. Under the umbrella of Mennonite Central Committee alone, private groups of churches helped over 4000 persons from the crowded camps of southeast Asia find a new life in Canada.

The Friesen Family Farm and the supporting congregation at Stratton, Ontario extended a helping hand most generously. Records at Mennonite Central Committee show that in six applications they sponsored 20 refugees from August, 1979 to July, 1982. Phu Sam was the single male in the first group to arrive at Stratton with a sister and three cousins. We are indeed pleased to see this personal story as prepared by Evelyn Friesen, one of the Friesen daughters, who observed the frustrations faced by these new Canadians in adjusting to our strange culture. Her recording of the experiences that brought Phu Sam and his friends to the point of risking their lives to gain freedom help us to understand their motivation and persistence. This story will be eagerly read by all who shared a part in the refugee saga as well as by others who may be wondering about the presence of the growing number of southeast Asians in our midst.

Frank Isaak
Former MCC Manitoba
Refugee Assistance Co-ordinator

FOREWORD

This book is the true account of a young Vietnamese refugee who immigrated to Canada in 1979. Some details have been changed to preserve identities. Other minor details have been added to fill in missing parts.

It is my desire that this book will help the reader to see refugees, in this case Vietnamese refugees, as individuals with personal struggles, as well as physical and emotional needs. Each refugee has a unique story to tell.

Evelyn Friesen

PREFACE

In spite of the love and care of our parents we want to grow and move out of their realm of influence. As time moves on we become older, change, and have to struggle for our own living. Once in a while our childhood experiences come back to our memory.

When I was a child I vaguely perceived the concept of FREEDOM. Nobody ever defined it for me. I never realized how much freedom I had until it was taken away from me.

When South Vietnam was defeated by North Vietnam, numerous people from the South fled the country because their freedom was taken away. A tragedy of the decade began. Nearly half of those who attempted to escape failed to reach their destination. Many thousands of helpless men, women and children ended up in the bottom of the angry ocean or in the hands of inhumane Thai pirates. This happened to innocent people in search of freedom.

Was it too high a price for these people to pay in order to repossess their once-owned freedom? History will be the judge of all these deeds.

I would like to give special thanks to Evelyn Friesen who has worked hard to put this book together and to the Friesen family for supporting our group in our first year in Canada. A special thanks as well to the government of Canada and other sponsoring groups who have generously allowed and helped many refugees to settle in this great country.

Phu Sam

TABLE OF CONTENTS

1. "I Passed!" 1
2. "The War is Over" 11
3. "I'm Going to Quit Running" 23
4. "I Feel so Much Hatred" 31
5. "Maybe I'm the One Who's Wrong" 37
6. "I have Someone to Live For" 45
7. "What About Escaping?" 55
8. "If We can Only get to Sea . . ." 65
9. "It's Time to Say Good-bye" 75
10. "Tomorrow will bring Us Freedom" 87
11. "Where Shall We Go?" 99
12. "Welcome to Canada" 113
13. "Now You have Five More Children" 119
14. "I'm back in school" 129
15. "Their God must have told Them to Sponsor Us" . 139
16. "We Want to Thank You" 149
17. "I have a Confession to Make" 153
18. "We're Becoming Independent" 163
19. "Thank you God, for bringing My Wife" 169
20. "It's Wonderful to be Free" 177

1

"I PASSED!"

Young Nam Tran sauntered along a shaded sidewalk in crowded, beautiful Saigon, the capital of South Vietnam, on his way home from school. It was nearly five o'clock, and the streets were a confusion of rushing cars, motorcycles, bicycles and buses. Throngs of people pushed by on foot.

It was a lovely April afternoon, the beginning of the rainy season, and the moderate temperature was a welcome change from the recent stiflingly hot weather.

Yet Nam noticed nothing of his surroundings. He was completely engrossed in thoughts of his academic progress.

"Oh I am so glad this day is over," he sighed. "Lately I've been swamped with my studies." Not only did Nam take the regular grade nine course, he also attended classes at a private high school in order to qualify for the 'Brevet d'étude du Premier Cecle,' a French diploma.

"Well," he consoled himself, "at least there are only two more months before it's all over."

He groaned inwardly. "Except, that is, for the exams! All the regular courses *plus* the French course! Everyone tells me the exams are tough. I wonder what I need to worry about most, the high school material or the BEPC?"

Nam's pace gradually slowed. He stopped and peered into

a tree, plucking at its leaves carelessly. He looked almost comical standing there, with his strange haircut, short pantlegs and serious expression. "Your pants are so short it would take a dog three days to climb up to the hem," his friends teased him sometimes.

But Nam cared little about his appearance or the opinion of others. "I love nature," he mused, "and the way the clouds move slowly through the sky. Soon it seems as if the trees are moving instead of the clouds."

He stared, dreaming. "Let's see . . . the trees are countries . . . the leaves are people . . . and the clouds are the patient earth. The leaves help the trees grow, and in the same way the trees, when they are grown, help the leaves and give them a better chance to grow. All the energy is drawn from the earth. . . ."

"Nam!" called a deep voice from the street. "What are you doing?"

Startled, Nam turned abruptly. A beaming smile broke across his countenance. It was his father!

Nam realized he should have been home half an hour ago. "Here I am on the street, daydreaming," he muttered, ashamed. "I'll have to think of a good excuse fast!" On second thought he decided to be honest with his father. He jumped into the car and started to explain.

But it was not necessary. "My father isn't even listening," Nam noted. "He's in a world of his own just like I was." With that the boy settled down contentedly in the passenger seat to watch the traffic.

Mr. Tran was deep in thought. Suddenly, however, he glanced at Nam. A new realization swept over him. "My son is no longer a child. He is becoming a fine young man. I must spend more time with him. This is my chance to help him grow, to strengthen his beliefs and knowledge for the future."

Their drive home took them through a quiet street, one of the most beautiful areas of the city. Villas of the wealthy stood splendidly on both sides. Large tamarind trees touched to form a cool, green vault over the avenue. Cicadas chirped noisely, unseen, in the branches above.

The shrill sound of the insects reminded Nam of the season and the fact that the school year would soon be over. It made him pensive again.

"The cicadas sing innocently in the air," he reflected. "Everyone interprets their song differently. To some graduates it's a song of sadness . . . to others it's a song of joy, announcing the coming of the holidays. For me . . . well, for me it's a song of both emotions. A great vacation awaits me, but it will mean a long period without my friends. Ah yes, soon I will leave the familiar old school where I grew up, where I enjoyed laughter — and suffered punishments!

"Before I know it, my friends will be scattered to every corner of the world. Some will stay in Saigon if they're lucky enough to get jobs, but most will go overseas for further education. Imagine, some of my friends may even become the political leaders of our country! Probably most will be just ordinary citizens though. . . . Hmm, I wonder what I'll be when I grow up? 'Que sera, sera,' that's all I can say. . . .

"Hey, are we home already? Am I ever a dreamer today! Father's already in the house, and I didn't even notice him pull into the driveway!"

Laughing, Nam flung open the car door and ran to the house.

* * *

For ten years people from all parts of Vietnam had been converging on the city of Saigon. The war had forced them to abandon their homes and property in the country and to settle in the teeming capital. Most of the arrivals were farmers without a trade or other skills, but they still preferred the problems of the city to the immediacy, fear, and upheavals of warfare.

By 1974 the city of 1,845 square kilometers held approximately three-and-a-half million people. It was difficult for newcomers to find a decent place to live. To complicate the housing situation, all the large buildings were occupied by army units from at least six different countries.

Although most street fronts were given to business, the

alleys, located approximately every hundred meters apart, were lined with houses. For most people these alleys were their passageway from one area to another; and it was these alleys that caused concern for many travellers. Nearly every alley had a band of young people who loitered about, watching for strangers. Frequently they would irritate the pedestrians until a fight erupted. Sometimes the gangs would attack and steal.

Nam lived in one of these alleys. Although the youth in his neighborhood were notorious for their fighting, Nam was still too young and too innocent to be a gang member. Besides, some would have thought him too educated. He was well-known however, and was not molested. Most people had great respect for his father.

Mr. Tran had a successful military career, and was at one time the premier of one of Vietnam's southern provinces. Mrs. Tran had owned two restaurants in the suburbs. The children attended one of the most prestigious schools in the country.

Nam sometimes wondered why his father insisted on living in a lower class area when they were considered a middle class family. No amount of complaining about the neighborhood could convince Mr. Tran to change his mind however.

"He probably wants to teach us more about life by integrating us with hard-working families," Nam reasoned. "Perhaps he wants us to recognize how difficult it really is to get ahead in society. Success takes a lot of hard work."

The remaining days of the school year passed quickly for Nam, and soon only a week remained before the BEPC examination. He studied with a passion, stopping only to sleep. He knew that a failure would bring embarrassment to his father. He worked to the point of forgetfulness.

He studied even while eating. Once he filled up a bowl of food and then left it standing while he returned to his bedroom to continue his review. By the time his stomach reminded him that he had missed a meal it was too late: his mother had cleaned away his dinner.

On the day of the exam, Nam entered the examination room fearful and agitated. His hands were moist with perspiration, his feet were cold.

"I know I've studied enough," he told himself firmly. "I should have no problems. It's probably the two French teachers supervising us and walking about that make me so nervous."

Slowly Nam regained his confidence. He wrote steadily and finished his paper a few minutes ahead of the time limit. He was surprised and relieved that he had been able to complete the exam, for it was long and a third of the students had not had enough time to finish.

That night Nam could not sleep. He tossed and turned in his bed. He wanted to go downstairs to check the time. The night seemed endless. He counted from one to one hundred, more than a hundred times. Then he tried to visualize all the sheep legs in a flock on a meadow. But nothing helped. He was still wide awake.

How could he sleep? The exam was over, yes, but the next day would be even more traumatic than today had been. Tomorrow the results of the examinations would be posted. It would be either his day of glory or his day of doom.

"What if my name is not on the list?" he imagined. "It would be my end. I'm not going to write the exam again, that's for sure. If I failed, I will run away from home. Maybe I'll even kill myself." He knew he could not bear the disappointment of his parents.

"Father has put a lot of money and time and effort into my education. I've tried my best to make good on that investment . . . but if I fail, that's it. Then it's because I'm not capable. The effort was there. Maybe I'm not smart enough. Maybe I'll never be as successful as my father."

Nam's mind would not rest: hour after hour he mulled over his uncertainties and dread. Finally he determined to convince himself that there was no good reason why he had not passed the exam. "I'm smart," he said, "and I've been working hard. I was well prepared. I will pass! I will receive the compliments of my family and friends. They are counting on me, and I won't let them down. I will be my father's successor. Tomorrow will be a victorious day for me. I'll go to church to thank God for giving me the confidence I needed while writing the paper. And, I'll have a long and enjoyable vacation. . . ."

Nam woke suddenly, terrified. His father was shaking his shoulder.

"Wake up, Nam. Wake up," Mr. Tran was saying.

Immediately the emotions of the night rushed over Nam. Today he must accompany his father to search for his name on the list of exam results. Had he passed? What if his name were not there? What would he do?

"Come on, Son, it's time to get up and get ready. I'll be waiting downstairs," ordered Mr. Tran in a low voice.

Nam felt sick with anxiety. He dressed quickly and swallowed a glass of milk for his breakfast.

Father and son rode silently in the car. Nam could scarcely contain the tension and excitement within him as they sped along the quiet avenues, along the familiar route to the school.

Approaching the building they saw a crowd of people surrounding the bulletin board where the results were posted. There was jostling and struggling as each tried to break through the wall of people to scrutinize the lists. They heard shrieks of excitement. Nam also sensed sadness. Some students had not found their names on the list. They probably hoped against hope that it was only a mistake, but still they knew that they had likely failed.

"Look," Mr. Tran commented, "some jump for joy, and others steal quickly away, wanting no one to see them and label them as failures. Well, that's life. We can't all be winners."

A surge of hope bounded through Nam's body. "I'm not going to be part of the quiet group. I'm going to be a winner."

Nam stepped out of the car, his face glowing with assurance, but his legs moving cautiously, as if to prepare for failure. Mr. Tran, however, strode briskly and impatiently through the crowd to the bulletin board. With a rapid glance he found his son's name. He felt relief, but he carefully controlled his reaction because he wanted Nam to have the privilege of finding his name first. He turned to look for Nam, and saw that the boy was having difficulty getting forward. In an authoritative voice he called, "Nam, come over here!" People cleared the way for Nam.

"D-did you find my name?" Nam faltered.

"You'll have to look for yourself," Mr. Tran replied.

Nam's eyes would scarcely focus on the list. There . . . Nam Tran. He blinked and looked again.

"Guess what?" he whooped to anyone who cared to hear. "I passed! I knew it would be there! Yeh!"

He jumped ecstatically and clapped his hands. He scarcely noticed the crowd push him away from the board and out of the way. He ran to his father and embraced him.

"I made it, Father!" he cried.

"Congratulations, Son!" Mr. Tran patted him on the shoulder. "I'm truly proud of you."

"Thanks. I wouldn't have made it without your support."

"Come on, Nam, let's go tell your mother. And then, let's celebrate!"

"Okay! I'll call some of my friends too."

"Good idea," Mr. Tran encouraged.

"It will be great to celebrate," Nam thought. "I worked hard; I put in a lot of effort. But just knowing I passed is the greatest reward I could have!"

"Now that you've made it this far," Mr. Tran said, "let's talk about your future. I want you to study hard the next few years in high school and get good grades so you'll qualify for a scholarship to take your post-secondary education overseas — maybe in France or Australia. All the French and English courses you've taken will be in your favor when you attend university abroad."

"I think I'm doing pretty good with my French and English," Nam reminded his father. "Remember the time your French-Canadian business friend called by phone? First he started talking in French. Naturally I replied in French. Then he switched to English. He was amazed that I could carry on a conversation in English too."

"I know," Mr. Tran said approvingly. "He found that surprising. You've got tremendous linguistic abilities, Son. Keep it up. I'm willing to invest a lot of money into your education."

Nam was determined to please his father and fulfill his wishes. "And what I can do today, I won't leave for tomorrow," he decided. He registered for several summer courses. His school break was busy and short.

Nam had one week of vacation before the regular school year commenced. He packed some clothes and boarded the bus for the two-hour trip to Tay Ninh, a province northwest of Saigon, to visit his grandfather and aunts.

"Ah, this will be great," Nam murmured, relaxed, as the bus left Saigon. "Life in the country must be wonderful compared to that of the city." He found enormous pleasure in the beauty of the countryside as the bus whizzed along the highway. The water in the rice pads reflected the magnificent blue sky with its scattered clouds.

Crops in Vietnam, a tropical country, could be planted year round. The rice fields were in various stages. On some pads the plants were beginning to sprout while on others the farmers were finishing their harvest operations. They would then burn the straw and use the ashes as fertilizer before the field would be seeded and flooded again.

"Why is this land divided into small sections separated by dikes?" Nam wondered. "Why wouldn't they cultivate a big field so that more space could be utilized? Why do people build barriers between themselves?"

The bus stopped frequently, at designated points, or even along the highway if the driver decided there was room for more passengers. The crew consisted of a driver and an assistant, usually a young man, in charge of loading and unloading the baggage. "That job looks interesting," Nam thought, "I'd like a job like that too."

Some fifty kilometers before Tay Ninh, Nam saw Bà-Den, the famous kilometer-high mountain of Vietnam. Its peak was crowned with surveillance equipment used to detect enemy movements in the area. It was a stark reminder to Nam that his country was still at war. It had been so all his life.

The presence of Philippine, Korean and Thai allied forces in Tay Ninh created excellent business opportunities for the townspeople. Since Tay Ninh lay on the border of Vietnam and Cambodia a large American base was also located there.

Transportation in the country was mostly by motorcycle and bicycle. Few owned cars. Military jeeps and trucks, however, were seen everywhere in the small country towns, transferring supplies and equipment to the front lines.

Nam's week in the country not only made him more mindful of the war, but also provided him with new experiences and understanding. He stayed with his retired grandfather. His three aunts worked for the government so Nam spent many hours with the boys his own age.

He rode the backs of his cousins' cows and chased them around the fields. He walked to the river, fifty meters from his grandfather's house. Once he swam after a duck. He swam so far that he had to walk back.

Another time he imitated his new friend and climbed a coconut tree. He got halfway up and then couldn't get down.

"We're not helping you," the boys teased. "You're old enough and smart enough to figure it out on your own." The boys left him hanging on the tree for half an hour before they finally assisted him down.

"Being here has changed my opinion about country people," Nam confessed to the boys. "Things which seem impossible for me are easy for you. I used to think you were just a bunch of uneducated kids. Now I've learned that you haven't had the opportunity to go to school, but you sure are smart enough. You know more tricks than I've ever known!"

Nam enjoyed cycling along the country roads. "How I love listening to the birds chirping! I love breathing this fresh, clean air. I love seeing nature. Life here is so peaceful," he exulted.

At the end of that week Nam reluctantly packed his bags to return to Saigon. "This is the best vacation I've ever had, Grandfather," Nam said. "I enjoyed the outdoors and learned new things about life and other people. Hopefully it will help me live more harmoniously with people and nature."

Travelling home, Nam reviewed the summer. "It's been terrific," he concluded. He had passed the examinations, he had worked hard on furthering his educational goals, and he had had a wonderful, if brief, holiday. He was young, energetic, and confident. The future looked bright.

Little did Nam realize how soon and how drastically his life would change.

2

"THE WAR IS OVER"

It was April again, one year later, 1975. Again Nam was strolling home from school, reliving the events of his day. He had now completed his grade ten studies. He was glad that he had only two more years left to finish his high school education.

"Some of my classmates sure acted strangely today," he recalled. "They were saying farewell to everyone, saying they wouldn't be back next year. It sounded as if they planned to go away, but it all seemed so vague. There was such an air of secrecy about it all."

In the last few months the Vietnamese war had taken, in Nam's opinion, some puzzling and grim twists. South Vietnam was living under martial law now; a curfew was in effect from eleven at night to five in the morning. Many more people had fled to Saigon, hoping to be safe.

Reports coming in about the battles were disturbing. By the third week of April all forty-four of South Vietnam's provinces had fallen or were encircled. Saigon alone was unconquered, alone against the enemy.

"It seems that wherever our soldiers fight, they lose," Nam grumbled to himself. "What a shame to see so many of them getting killed. The Americans have withdrawn their financial support, leaving us helpless and powerless. This seems a lot worse than our last big battle in 1972."

On April 23, U.S. President Gerald Ford had called the Vietnamese conflict "finished."

"Today America can regain a sense of pride that existed before Vietnam," he had declared. "But it cannot be regained by refighting a war that is finished as far as America is concerned."

Had the United States, North Vietnam and South Vietnam reached an agreement? Nobody seemed to know.

Nam was young and had lived his few years against the background of the long war between the two Vietnams. He had followed the news, but it had not affected him much. War was a normal situation. Now, however, there was a new mood in Saigon that gripped him with terror.

"What's happening?" he wondered desperately. "Is this just another uprising, just something that will soon settle down? Will this be the last battle, finally, the last time our people will have to fight?

"I feel terribly insecure about it all," he admitted to himself. "With the way things are now I don't see how South Vietnam can regain her territory. And what kind of an agreement will be possible with the weakness and disarray of our government?"

He recollected vividly the shock he had experienced when he heard President Nguyen Van Thieu on national television on April 21, bitterly accusing the United States of having abandoned South Vietnam and then announcing his resignation from office.

Nam had sat in unbelieving silence for the next half hour, trying to sort out what had transpired. "So this *is* the end," he had realized numbly. "The war is over. President Ford is right. What will happen now? Soon there will be no South Vietnam left. The courageous soldiers still fighting will soon be out of supplies. They deserve honor for resisting to the end, but they'll likely soon be forgotten."

As the days of that unhappy April passed, Nam observed and felt deeply the events of history playing themselves out around him. He felt sure that the military leaders of the country would be able to find a solution, but even they seemed stricken with panic. Many of the high-ranking officers abandoned their posts; the soldiers were left without leadership. They had not learned to make their own decisions.

Thousands of people bought their way out of the country on commercial air flights. By the time the city was surrounded by enemy forces and facing the final ultimatum of the North, many of the rich and influential were gone.

After president Thieu's resignation, vice-president Huong took power for several days, and then the presidency was transferred to General Duong Van Minh.

People seemed to be leaving constantly. Vietnam was not considered safe anymore. The Tran family watched and became increasingly apprehensive as they heard of one neighbor after another fleeing the country.

Mr. Tran ordered his family to be ready to evacuate momentarily as well. Mrs. Tran packed a handbag with changes of clothing for her husband and herself and each of the five children. The girls prepared packages of dry food. Nam's responsibility was to gather everyone's birth certificate. "We could be evacuating anytime," Mr. Tran reminded the family as they scurried to pack.

During the next days thousands of people thronged to the airport. They squeezed desperately through small holes in the fence in order to reach a plane. Others climbed over fences and trees. Police guards shot at those attempting to enter illegally but it did not deter the panic-stricken crowd.

"We want out!" was the cry as people stumbled over dead bodies piling up along the fence. Their only desire was to reach the planes that could take them out of the country. Some planes crashed shortly after takeoff due to overloading.

There seemed no time to waste. "Now is the time to leave," many cried as they ran along the streets leaving friends and family members behind.

At the river ports people screamed and shouted for help. Crowds pushed rashly towards the boats, knocking down some of those who were already standing in the water.

While many people searched frantically for a means of escape, others capitalized on the confusion to loot cars, motorcycles and other abandoned possessions. Some fortune hunters even instructed their children to crawl through small holes into warehouses at the dock and throw out to the adults anything they could find inside. Those who fled for freedom were too distraught to care what happened behind their backs.

During the night of April 29, the enemy forces obliterated the airport. That day and until the following morning a tense and hurried final evacuation of foreign and high-ranking Vietnamese personnel took place in Saigon. Helicopters landed on the rooftops of embassies to pick up diplomats.

Many Vietnamese managed to squeeze through the gates of these buildings, past the armed guards, and up to the roofs. Unfortunately many of them were pushed off the terraces. Their screams of agony could be heard over the city.

But their cries did not deter other Vietnamese from risking their lives for freedom. In desperation some clung to the helicopter landing bars until they could not hold on any longer and were wrenched loose, falling to their deaths as the helicopters whizzed through the air. It seemed as if no one cared.

Meanwhile, the battle front moved progressively closer to Saigon. Indeed, the Communists seemed to be everywhere. They were close to their goal of conquering the South, and they would not give up now.

As the sun set on April 29, the evacuation procedures continued, and intensified. Hundreds of helicopters swarmed over the city like giant locusts ascending from different parts of the city and heading due east to an American fleet of forty ships waiting off the coast in the South China Sea.

The enemy drew still nearer, and in some parts of the city began firing at the evacuation planes. Nam watched the scene from the rooftop of their two-storey house. He saw red burning bullets dancing into the sky from anti-aircraft equipment on the ground. Most of the helicopters were piloted by experienced professionals who managed to weave through the rain of bullets. Some planes exploded with bright flames, but still the evacuation went on.

"Why isn't Father doing anything?" Nam muttered as he followed the battle in the air. "Everyone else goes crazy about leaving and we sit at home as if nothing is happening! I just can't understand why he is so optimistic. He keeps saying the war will stop soon. He says an agreement has been reached by the three governments involved."

That night Mr. Tran calmed his family with these same assurances and they all went to bed hopeful for a better tomorrow.

The following morning, April 30, 1975, Nam awoke to the steady drone of the helicopters proceeding with evacuation and of shooting from every part of the city. "Thousands of people must have been killed by now," he concluded as he surveyed the city from the rooftop again. Most of the wealthy people from their area had left; on many streets most of the houses were vacant.

Mrs. Tran was greatly perturbed about her husband's indifference. "Aren't you going to do anything about this situation?" she pleaded in tears. "The Communists are at the back yard and you pretend nothing has happened!"

"I already told you, everything is going to be fine," Mr. Tran repeated firmly. "We don't need to go anywhere. As I said, a cease-fire agreement has been reached. Soon everything will be all right. I'd really rather stay here than leave our dear country. You know how difficult it would be to live overseas. There we would have to start over. We'd face discrimination. I've been in the United States and I don't think I would like to live there at all."

Mr. Tran paused for a minute, and then said slowly, "But, it's up to you to decide. If you want to go I'll contact some friends and we'll leave later today. But I still love it here. This is my home, and nothing can replace home. You too were born and raised here."

"I know you're right," Mrs. Tran admitted reluctantly. "This is our homeland, this is where we were raised, but still, I don't want to see my children growing up in a communist society. In a few hours the Communists may take over. The future of our children is in jeopardy. Look how much money and time you have invested in your children's education. What will that help them under the Communists? Would Nam be able to go to university? Would he be able to become whatever he wants? What about the girls? I don't want to see them suffer. And what about you? Would they let you go free? You've been working with the Americans and in our government.

"How would I raise the family alone?" Mrs. Tran continued emotionally. "You never let me do anything. It's about time I decide my future and the future of my children. If you want to stay, stay, but take me and the children somewhere where we can leave Vietnam." Her words were anguished.

Nam listened to his parents debate and wondered with whom he should side. The views of both seemed valid, but he was distressed to hear them argue.

He quickly attempted to help. "Mother," he said, "we can go at anytime. Why don't you ask the girls to fix dinner and Father can make arrangements for our departure later in the day."

"Nam is right," Mr. Tran agreed. "Let's have dinner a little earlier than usual. I promise to complete our evacuation arrangements this afternoon."

Mrs. Tran was disappointed that they would not leave immediately, but she realized she could not alter the decision. She went to the kitchen to prepare the next meal.

When she was gone Nam turned to his father anxiously. "Are you sure a cease-fire will be reached, Father?" he asked. "By the way things look I think it's too late. The Communists are so aggressive they won't stop now. We Southerners are too weak to defend ourselves. The Americans have left their embassy; they're abandoning us. Who is going to help us get out of this dilemma? Everywhere I go, I see soldiers running away, dropping their uniforms. They're like snakes without heads now that their leaders have fled. I don't see any reason why the North would back out. I don't know when they'll take over, but surely they'll do it shortly."

"Well Son, you could be right," Mr. Tran said amiably. "I have nothing against your opinion, but I have my information from a reliable source."

Mr. Tran leaned toward Nam in a confidential manner. "You see, the Americans are just setting up a trap. The Communists won't be able to make it. At any moment American help will be sent in from Thailand or the fleets to recover the South. I believe they're just waiting for the perfect moment. I'm confident they will do it."

Nam didn't want to contend with his father, but he couldn't agree with him either. "I see what you mean," he said, "but you may be mistaken. What do the Americans want with this place? There's nothing here for them to exploit. It just doesn't make sense for them to come back."

He paused a second, then added respectfully, "I guess I could be wrong too."

Nam, noticing his father thinking seriously, ran back up to the rooftop. He observed that very few American aircraft were left. Apparently they had nearly completed the evacuation of their staff and the Vietnamese who helped them.

A sudden feeling of sadness engulfed Nam as he realized that he was watching the last Americans leaving his country. He was witnessing the end of an era, and what seemed to him to be the death of his lively and lovely city of three-and-a-half million people.

"I wish I was sitting in one of those helicopters," Nam said disconsolately. "My mind goes blank when I try to sort it all out."

He thought of the golden days when the American soldiers were everywhere on the streets of Saigon. They dispensed chewing gum to children. Their convoys slowed traffic on the highways. They sat on the backs of their trucks drinking beer, laughing and joking.

"Now our American friends — oh, are they really our friends? — are leaving us without even saying goodbye. They're in a great hurry, trying to avoid trouble or death. To them the whole experience must be a nightmare too.

"For some of us this was our best time — we had a chance to get rich and enjoy American luxuries. Maybe that's why we lost the war? People were too busy enjoying life to bother fighting for our country. Now we'll have to live with the consequences of a costly mistake.

"Our soldiers fought because they were forced to," Nam agonized. "They had no goals of their own and they haven't accomplished anything either. Who is to blame? How will history view it all? Was it because of Vietnam's leaders or the Americans?

"I shouldn't worry about this. I'm too young to worry about politics," Nam told himself. "I don't know much about it to begin with and I don't expect to ever find the answers to all my questions. I might as well forget my confusion and pretend everything is fine."

After dinner Mr. Tran took his usual afternoon nap. He closed the windows to block off outside noise and turned on the air conditioner.

"Dad seems so calm," Nam said into his pillow as he too tried to rest. "I wish I could relax like he does and shut out all that's happening. Maybe I can't sleep because it's so hot in here . . . . I'm going downstairs to listen to the radio. I don't want to miss the news."

Nam turned on the radio.

"What did they say?" he gasped. "Did I hear something about surrender? Who? Surrender?"

He froze, his hand still on the volume switch. The announcement was repeated.

"The South has surrendered! The North is taking over."

At eleven that morning the flag of the Provisional Revolutionary Government had been raised at Saigon's presidential palace, and in his last act as president of South Vietnam, General Duong Van Minh had broadcast an order to his troops. "Lay down your arms and surrender unconditionally," he had commanded. He was then arrested and led away.

Nam burst into his father's bedroom.

"The South has surrendered!" he cried out. "The North is taking over."

Mr. Tran jumped up, startled and confused.

"W-w-what?" he stammered.

"It's true. They're repeating the message over and over on the radio. The South has surrendered."

"I don't believe it," Mr. Tran protested. "I won't believe it until I hear it myself."

When Mrs. Tran heard the news she broke down in tears.

"I told you so!" she lashed out at her husband. "Why didn't you listen? Now we're as good as dead! We'll be persecuted by those cruel Communists. There go our dreams, our future! Here comes hardship and depression!"

"If only you had listened to Mother and us children," Nam wanted to add. But he saw the disappointment in his father's face. Mr. Tran had been betrayed.

Fear gripped Mr. Tran and he began pacing the floor. "I guess I was wrong," he said brokenly. "I was so confident that we'd win. What will the Communists do to me? And how are you going to survive? I've put all my money into the bank and into business. I have no cash on hand."

Mr. Tran realized he had to take immediate action. He could not let his family down again. He had to be brave and suppress his fears. Quickly he ordered his family to gather all the records and pictures of his involvement with the previous regime. They spent the rest of the day burning the papers.

But the next day the Tran family learned that several people on their street were undercover Communists.

In a matter of a few days Mr. Tran aged a couple of years. He stayed up late at night, worrying.

"He's going through terrible mental stress," Nam thought sympathetically. "All his life he's worked hard. He built up dreams for our future. Now he's only halfway through life, and our country has fallen and he feels guilty for not listening to the rest of the family. He was too confident. Now he suffers. Oh, how I hate to see that dark look on his face."

Nam knew there were probably many Vietnamese people who were feeling the same shock and sorrow as his father was. "They sacrificed their lives to keep the South free from the Reds. They did it in vain," he thought angrily. "They've been betrayed. They shed innocent blood over some stupid ideology. Who really gained in this war? The North? They won, sure, but what did they achieve? Now they have a chaotic country with a deficient economy on their hands."

Over and over Nam struggled with the issues of the war and its distressing end. "Should it even have been fought in the first place?" he wondered. "Couldn't the political leaders have come to a peaceful solution years ago? Something that would have made our nation, with its thousand years of pride and heritage, a strong and competent nation?

"We're not stupid people! We fought to keep our country free from foreign intruders but ended up fighting each other. Now the North Vietnamese, the winners, self-righteously condemn us, the South Vietnamese, the losers."

The new communist government tried to pacify the South. They proclaimed, "We are all Vietnamese. The government will forgive and forget what the South Vietnamese have done."

Officers and civil workers of the former regime were called to various stations around the country to study government policies. It was to help them cope with the new society. Many were forced to convince themselves to be patriotic toward the new rulers.

"We will not avenge anyone for what has been done," the government announced. "Everyone who worked under the previous regime will study new government policies for ten days in various camps. Then they will return to rebuild the country."

Before a month had passed most of the people's hearts were won by an illusive promise of a quick recovery.

Mr. Tran was one of the many men called to a re-education center. But he did not return after ten days.

All over the country family members were outraged when their husbands, fathers, sons and brothers were not released from the re-education camps. But there was nothing they could do about it. Fighting against the new system only made the consequences that much worse.

3

"I'M GOING TO QUIT RUNNING"

With their father gone and his wealth and assets worthless, one basic, powerful need confronted the Tran family: simple survival. Eldest son Nam felt deeply the burden of responsibility that now rested on his sixteen-year-old shoulders.

Nam was a sensitive, intelligent person, but he found it difficult to express his emotions. Yet they spoke, unbidden, within himself constantly. He struggled to accept the turns life had taken and the reversal of his dreams. He resented the new regime. Never had he known, when it was his, how precious freedom was: it was not something tangible he could define even now, and yet in its loss he felt that everything he once had was altered or gone. He was confused and full of grief. But he dared not indulge it outwardly. He had a duty to help his family.

The Trans first tried their hand at the trading business. As long as Nam could remember his mother had been in the trading business, dealing in gold and diamonds for personal use and gain. Nam now began to trade with anything he could procur.

Bicycles were the country's most popular means of transportation, and so the Tran family opened a bicycle booth at the marketplace. Mrs. Tran and her four daughters handled the selling of parts and bicycles at the stall while Nam scurried about the city to buy more parts and assemble bicycles at home. With practice he became quite efficient; unfortunately, however, business at the booth decreased with the rise of inflation. Prices were gauged by demand and changed everyday. Another setback was that much of the business was controlled by the Chinese population in Saigon. Nam did not understand the Chinese language.

By summer Nam was restless. He confronted his mother. "We're obviously not making any headway with our bicycle business," he said. "My friend Minh and I are going to the country to see if we can earn something by selling monkeys and squirrels. We'll buy them and re-sell them as pets."

After several days of selling monkeys and squirrels Minh suggested they trap their own animals in the bush to increase their profits. They set out for the forest.

The weather was cold and damp. They often ran just to keep warm. They ran downhill and when approaching an incline tried to hop a ride on a vehicle. This greatly annoyed the drivers but when they stopped to chase them off Nam and Minh jumped down safely and ran.

The boys usually stayed with Minh's father at night even though he lived in extreme poverty. The only shelter he had was a roof. The boys slept on benches without blankets, shivering and scarcely sleeping.

Early one morning Minh nudged Nam. "Good morning, Nam! I've got an idea."

"We could use an idea because we haven't made any money so far," Nam grumbled, rubbing the tiredness out of his eyes.

"Why don't we go for a hike up that hill? There's a huge banana plantation ready for harvesting. There's bound to be monkeys in there."

"Sounds all right, Minh. I could use a bunch of bananas myself right now. Let's get going before the farmers chase all the monkeys away."

An hour later they reached their destination, panting from exertion and feeling ravenously hungry.

They scanned the plantation. "This wasn't such a great idea after all," Minh admitted. "No monkeys and not that many bananas either!"

"At least we found enough to fill our growling stomachs," Nam said. He ran his fingers through his dishevelled hair. "Well, what'll we do now? No luck with trapping. I can't afford to stay in the country. But I don't want to return to the city either. Not until I can take some earned money back with me."

He took a step forward. "Come on, let's walk through that bush. Maybe we'll come up with another bright idea!"

"You know what?" Minh suggested somewhat reluctantly. "I'm thinking maybe we should just go home. We can't find anything to do here."

"I was afraid he'd get that idea," Nam thought. He turned to his friend. "I know we don't have anything to do here, Minh, but at least we're free to do what we want. I just don't feel ready to be in the city again. I don't know exactly why . . . ."

They walked in silence, each involved with his own thoughts.

"I'm mixed up about it all," Nam analyzed. "I have a feeling I should go back to the city. I don't want to though. . . . I want an answer, especially for the questions I have when I walk past those war shelters. I pity those soldiers. I pity this country. I pity our people and my family and myself . . ."

Not knowing what to do the boys finally sat down in a corner of the plantation. The ground was soft and muddy from the night's rain.

"Who cares if it's wet?" Nam said as he stretched out on the damp earth. "Look at those birds enjoying the morning sun! They sound so happy. I guess they don't know what happened to our country. I wish I was a bird."

Then Nan heard voices in the distance. He listened and could understand snatches of the conversation. It seemed to be a group of farmers taking a mid-morning break.

"They're so busy with their work they don't have time to think about what is what either. All they care about is the weather and the crops."

Suddenly Nam jumped up. "Minh, you're right. Let's go home. There's nothing worth staying here for."

"Okay, but don't you dare change your mind," Minh declared.

"I won't."

The boys took another road to avoid the farmers, who might not be pleased at two teenagers loitering on their property. They ran until they were tired, and at last ended up in an open field where they discovered an underground war shelter.

"Let's explore!" Minh called.

They held on to the walls of the entrance as they inched apprehensively into the shelter. Then through the darkness they could faintly see bones. They froze. Shivers rippled over their bodies.

"I feel the ghostly blackness of horror," Nam shuddered.

"This cave is filled with human bones," Minh whispered.

"They're the remains of our soldiers killed during the war," Nam added. "Let's get out of here. This makes me sick."

"What good did all the killing do?" Nam burst out angrily when they emerged from the shelter. "Our soldiers fought against communism with determination and confidence. But it seems so futile now."

They ran to the main highway. From there they walked back to the dwelling of Minh's father. They cleaned up and packed to return to Saigon.

At the highway Nam and Minh tried to catch a ride to the city. Any vehicle would do, as long as they could travel free. They did not have sufficient money to pay the fare.

"Everyone says we don't have enough money," Nam laughed, "but that isn't the real excuse. People just don't like to see this monkey hanging on my shoulder! It's six hours since we left your father's place and we still haven't managed to get a ride. I'm getting pretty tired. I hate the thought of staying here for another night —

"Hey Minh, did you see that truck pull up? They're unloading people and merchandise. Take this monkey and I'll run and make arrangements for a ride to the city."

"Are you going to Saigon?" Nam called to the driver's assistant.

"Yes. If you want to ride it's six piastre per person."

"Can you wait a few minutes until my friend gets here?"

"Yes, but hurry up," the assistant warned. "It's getting late."

Nam scurried back to assist Minh with the monkey. "They want six piastre each for the ride. I have three piastre. How much money do you have?"

"Only three piastre too! Just a second . . . Here's another piastre in my pocket."

"We have only seven piastre. What do we do now?" Minh gasped as they raced toward the truck.

"Don't worry. I'll handle it." Nam tried to sound confident but he thought privately it would be closer to a miracle if they both got a ride on the truck. He quickly sent up a prayer.

"Hurry up boys," called the trucker's assistant. "We're all waiting. Here, let me help you on to the truck."

"Be careful. If you scare my monkey it will run away," Nam said.

Once on the truck Nam realized they had not been asked for their money. Hoping it would be forgotten, the boys moved to the front of the truck. If the assistant wanted the money he would have to scramble through all the boxes to reach them. Perhaps, Nam hoped, he would not bother.

"My guess was right," Nam told Minh as they approached the city. "He hasn't asked us for the money. Let's hope he forgets until we reach our destination."

The drivers' assistant hollered. "Where did you guys want to get off?"

"Not far from here, sir," Nam replied. His muscles tightened. "I'm afraid if he finds out we don't have enough money he might drop us off right where we are. It could take us a good five hours to walk home."

As if reading their thoughts one of the men called, "Have you guys got the money with you?"

"Yes, yes sir, we do." Nam handed him the rolled up bills.

The man counted the money. "Why only seven piastre?"

"Well," Nam hesitated, "you see . . ."

"See what?"

Nam could think of nothing to say. As if innocent he stared at the man.

"You guys cheated me," the trucker scowled. "I shouldn't have let you on in the first place."

"I'm sorry sir. I was going to tell you but I didn't have a chance when I got on the truck," Nam apologized.

"Okay. It's too late to do anything now, but remember next time I see you guys around, either you give me your money before you get on or you'll stay where you are. No more mercy for you. It's not easy to make a living nowadays, you know?"

"Oh, how well I *do* know," Nam thought. Aloud he said, "I'm sorry, sir. There won't be a second time."

"All right. Just tell me where you want to get off."

"Yes sir, we'll let you know," Nam promised.

How relieved Nam felt when he arrived home safely. His sisters were delighted with the little monkey, although his young brother Jean was afraid of it.

Nam went to bed early and slept soundly, glad to be in his own bed again. He was startled out of his sleep the next morning, however, by his mother shaking his roughly.

"Wake up, Nam. I have bad news."

Nam saw tears in his mother's eyes. "What's wrong?" he asked, alarmed.

"Your grandfather passed away last night."

"I don't understand!" Nam protested when he grasped

what his mother had said. "First my father is captured and then my grandfather dies. What will happen next? Grandfather was the healthiest person I've ever seen at the age of seventy-four. He chopped a cord of wood a day. He still had large firm muscles on the day the country fell into the hands of communism. He fell sick the day he heard that my father was captured. How deeply he loved my father!

"I think that's why he spent so much time with me after my father left. But his depression turned a healthy man into mere skin and bones in a matter of months."

At the funeral everyone was in tears except for Nam, yet he felt that nobody was in greater inner turmoil than he was.

"I just can't get myself to cry," he thought. "But I feel like doing something to avenge my grandfather's death. I'm sick and tired of living in this mass communist prison. But I'm powerless. What can I do by myself?

"With the two most important people in my life taken from me I have nothing left to live for. Depression and confusion is all I have. No dreams, goals or ideals. I don't even care anymore what happens."

Nam decided to return to the country, to his grandfather's community. Perhaps he could pay his last respects and find some comfort in knowing he was walking the ground his grandfather used to tread.

After being in the country for a week Nam observed that numerous country people made their living by raising chickens. It gave the enterprising lad another idea. He bought some roosters, of all kinds, and began to raise them for rooster fights. Some he took to the city and others he left with various friends in the country.

"I love watching roosters fight," he explained enthusiastically to his friends. "I fight the roosters too. Once I threw a shoe at a rooster. You should have seen him attack and demolish that shoe!"

Raising and selling roosters turned out to be more of a hobby than a profitable business, however. As September neared with its new school year Nam sold his birds and returned to school.

"As much as I hate the thought of studying under this perverted system, it's the only choice I have," he decided. "I'm only sixteen. I'm without the leadership of my father and grandfather. I've tried making a living and I've failed. I'll simply have to return to school, become indoctrinated and pretend everything is all right. I'll have to make the best of things. I'm going to quit running."

4

"I FEEL SO MUCH HATRED"

Pretending all was well proved impossible for Nam, however. His inner resistance soon showed itself in rebelliousness.

"Hey you guys, let's have a party at school tomorrow!" Nam suggested to his fellow grade eleven students one day.

"Sure! That would really get our politics teacher upset!" Hai agreed.

"Here's what we'll do," Nam stated to his four friends. "We'll all bring a bottle of beer to Mr. Nguyen's class and live it up. Let's make sure we disrupt the whole class before he has a chance to shove any of that New Regime garbage down our throats."

"A great idea!" Hai echoed. "But," he added, "we may be in for a lot of trouble one of these days."

The next morning Nam carefully wrapped a bottle of beer inside some newspaper. "I'm not sure I can trust those guys to go along with the plan. Just in case they back out, I'll keep this under cover."

"Did you bring your beer?" Nam's friends called when he arrived at school.

"I sure did!"

"Yippee!" they cheered.

"Can't you just picture Mr. Nguyen's reaction?" Hoan beamed in anticipation. "I can hear him screaming already."

"Quite frankly I don't care what he or anyone else says," Nam said boldly. "I've had enough of those communistic theories."

The school buzzer rang. The rowdy bunch marched into class.

"Here he comes!" warned Quoc, snickering. "Out with your bottles!"

"Anyone for some beer?" Nam said loudly, swaggering for effect. "It's party time!"

"Yeah!" cheered the students.

"What's going on?" Mr. Nguyen stormed into class. "Who do you think you are?" he shouted. "Get out of here, you with the beer!"

"Nonsense," retorted Nam calmly. "We need a break. We've had enough of your ridiculous educational system."

"I said to get out! Right now!" Mr. Nguyen stamped his feet in anger.

"See him get mad?" gloated the conspirators, sauntering throughout the classroom.

Several fellows joined them. They began to throw books and spill beer on each other.

Hearing the noise the principal rushed to the classroom. "What's this all about? Nam are you the leader of this again?" He ran towards Nam and attempted to grab him.

Mr. Nguyen stood at the door motionless, angry and bewildered.

"Head for the windows, you guys," Nam ordered.

They threw the bottles against the window panes. The glass shattered and tinkled to the floor. All five boys leapt out.

At a safe distance they stopped and caught their breath, panting and laughing. "We caused an uproar just like we planned," Hoan chuckled. "Now what?"

"Do you know we could be imprisoned for rebelling against communism?" Hai warned. His face grew serious as he realized what they had done.

"I know," Nam answered, "but what can we lose? Education? School isn't doing us any good, obviously . . . Oh, oh, here comes the principal."

"He can't do anything to us. We're the tallest and strongest guys in school," Hoan bragged. "He knows that."

"Let's just see what will happen," Nam instructed.

The principal walked to where the boys huddled under a tree. "You must be aware of the fact that your behavior today is not approved in our system," he began immediately. "Can you explain why you acted in this manner?"

"We were in the mood for celebrating," lied Hoan.

"Celebrating!" Nam thought bitterly. "What's there to celebrate? My father's in prison, and my grandfather died of depression. That's what came with the promise of a better future. They say they're re-educating my father. In the meantime there's no one in our family to earn a living. We have so many financial problems. Celebrate, sure! Injustice?"

"I'd better wake up," Nam checked his sarcasm. "The principal is waiting for a response from me."

"Uh, uh . . . I'm sorry about what happened," Nam searched for appropriate words. "I didn't know it is illegal to drink in school. Our list of regulations doesn't say anything about drinking."

"It will be your duty to clean up the mess in the classroom and to replace the broken windows. Let me assure you that if this happens again I will not hesitate to call the police," the principal said sternly. He turned and strode back to the school.

"Wow! Did you handle that well!" the boys complimented Nam.

That evening Nam continued to mull and search for answers. "I'm the oldest boy in my family so naturally the responsibility for my family's survival falls on me. And my father is the oldest in his family which means that his responsibility toward his family fell on me too when he was taken captive. And what am I doing about all these responsibilities? Mother can't get a job because father is considered a criminal.

Besides, she's busy enough with her housekeeping duties. My sisters and brother aren't getting enough to eat. I'd sure enjoy a decent full course meal myself for a change."

On an impulse Nam decided to talk to his older sister Phuong. He had often marvelled at her quiet spirit and contentment in spite of her poor health. Nam realized he had not respected her opinions as he should have.

He found his sister quite relaxed, studying her history text.

"How do you like our educational system, Phuong?" Nam asked.

"I don't like it, but there's no point in speaking against it. I certainly don't want to cause the kind of disturbance you caused today. I was terribly embarrassed when I heard about it," Phuong admonished.

"Maybe I didn't act very maturely, but don't you ever get upset? Can't you see what's happening to our family?" Nam responded.

"Yes Nam, I do get upset," Phuong said evenly, "but I enjoy studying. I love to study history and politics. As much as I disagree with the new regime, I refuse to speak against it at school. Don't you realize that could mean immediate imprisonment? I'm just not going to risk it. It's enough to have Father in prison."

The next morning Nam returned to school but his inner conflict remained unresolved. While in class he tuned out the lectures and reasoned with himself. "I don't know why, but whenever I'm in class I feel so much hatred. . . . I feel I could murder many people. . . . My parents want me to complete high school but I can't see any reason for staying in school. But I would feel guilty about dropping out because that would hurt them. But I have absolutely no motivation to complete grade eleven. . . .

"Communism says everyone has to be re-educated but all they're doing is brainwashing us. I don't need any of that. I'd be more useful if I got a job. . . ."

In November Nam announced to his mother that he was

going to drop out of school. "I'm sorry to go against your wishes," he said, "but I don't see how anyone will benefit from my being brainwashed in school while our family is starving."

Nam often wondered how his father felt about communism now. He speculated about what it was like in a re-education camp and how his Father was treated.

Nam knew that all those who had worked for the previous regime were in the camps to be indoctrinated with the politics of the new government. Besides attending courses, they generally worked eight-hour days, seven days a week, planting crops or toiling in the bush or raising farm animals. They were responsible to provide their own food on a limited allowance.

Mr. Tran wrote his family a letter occasionally, but the recipients knew the contents were carefully censored. All the letters actually told them was that he was alive. They did not reveal his real feelings, his state of health or his prison experiences.

Although Mr. Tran's prison was only thirty-two kilometers from his home, the family saw him perhaps two or three times a year. Their visits were closely monitored by prison guards and limited to one or two hours. The family was responsible to provide him with clothing and extra food on these rare occasions. Nam wished he could have even one private conversation with his father.

One adult member of each household also had to attend two weekly re-education meetings. This responsibility usually fell on either Nam or Phuong. They heard reports on global news and were instructed on attitudes to take towards other countries. Much to Nam's dislike everyone had to sign a promise to fight for communism at the end of each meeting.

"As if going to those meetings isn't enough," Nam complained to his mother one day when the census taker visited their house. "What business of theirs is it to come every month to record who lives in this house, what occupation we're in and when everyone's birthday happens to be? They seem to want more and more control over us all the time."

Mrs. Tran sighed. "I know it's getting worse all the time, Nam, but what can we do? All I can think of is to hope and pray for a better tomorrow."

5

"MAYBE I'M THE ONE WHO'S WRONG"

On Nam's next visit to his father he broke the news. "Father, I've dropped out of school. I found it too depressing."

"Why did you do that, my son?" Mr. Tran reproached him. "Don't you know that your mother and I have always wanted our children to get a good education? Why don't you go back and give it another chance?"

"For your sake I would do it, Father, but I can't. I'm not in the right frame of mind to go to school," Nam objected.

Nam returned home more perplexed then ever. "First I lose the guidance of my father and grandfather. They are the two people I most respected. Then when Father is able to give me his advice I reject it.

"What a terrible person I am," he thought guiltily. "My father has every right to blame me and get upset with me, but I refuse to return to school."

Nam searched for a job but nothing was available. He moved from home to friends' places and then back home again. His physical restlessness reflected the perpetual agitation of his inner life.

"Everywhere I go I meet up with darkness," he thought. "There's only trouble and misery ahead for my family. I've always prided myself on being able to find a solution for my problems but. . . ." He began to consider suicide.

"In trying to help my family I've only disappointed them by dropping out of school," he reflected gloomily one night. "Everyone can see that I'm just making a fool of myself and bringing shame to my parents. One of these days I'm going to end it all by jumping into the river before it drives me insane." The troubled teenager tossed and turned in anguish without sleeping.

Towards morning Nam reached a decision, one that almost startled him because it was something he had never expected to do. He would submit. He would expose himself thoroughly to re-education and keep his mind open.

"Maybe I'm making myself crazy by refusing to give communism a chance," he reasoned. "Maybe it's not as bad as I've thought . . . maybe I'm the one who's wrong."

It brought a curious sense of relief to Nam to cease resisting the changes that had occurred in Vietnam. Gradually life started looking brighter. He discovered strength within himself which he had not had when he felt so confused. He began to use his enormous energies and his mental abilities by participating in as many communist programs as possible. The hope that his family might benefit by his eagerness spurred him on.

Nam volunteered for adult education and got a job teaching older people to read. Next he got involved with young people's clubs. Their meetings would educate him in the communist political system.

Nam directed all his determination and enthusiasm toward work in the club. He had made up his mind and he would do it — the cause of communism must be furthered. He advanced quickly and was soon vice-president of the local group. He could have become president if it had not been for his father's status as a criminal.

"Boy, now you're a hot shot!" several people taunted. But criticism did not stop him.

"I don't care what others think," Nam thought. "I'm going

to carry out my plan and support our government no matter what my own beliefs and feelings are."

He took courses in public speaking, group management and public debating. He overcame his reticence and delivered convincing speeches on the streets.

"You all know that communism takes over farms," he said in his orations. "You've all heard of rich families who have been chased out of their homes during the middle of the night, able to take with them only a change of clothing.

"This may seem harsh but there is a reason for it! Those people thought they had worked hard all their lives and were rich as a result of their efficiency. That is a lie! The reason they are rich is because they cooperated with the Americans. That's how they got ahead! They could never have done it on their own. And in the process, they cheated the rest of us!

"Communism means equality. We can't let some people get by with false riches while others are poor.

"Here's an example of how the rich cheat the poor. Look at the factory owners in America. Let's say one thousand people are employed in a factory. If one employee arrives late a big fuss is made, but if each worker works five minutes longer than normal the managers are quiet. That's five thousand minutes of free work for the company. Thus the rich become richer and a gap in society is created. The rich become more powerful and manipulate the lower classes.

"You are poor because the rich cheat you constantly, one way or the other. So, it's only fair that the government chases the rich out of their luxurious homes. It's to help you!

"Communism believes in equality. One for all and all for one. And it's time to make the rich pay.

"You don't see the money that's taken because it's kept in the government bank to be dispensed evenly as the need arises. Remember it's equality we're fighting for.

"You might feel you're still not getting your share. That's because there are still private businesses that cheat you. We must confiscate all privately-owned property. Our slogan is: The public is the boss! The public owns all property! The government administers the property for the public. But in reality it's all yours."

Nam almost dreaded ending his lectures, for after the convincing words died away he was faced with the doubt of his own heart. He had tried to make himself too busy to think, and it had been good for him to be active again, yet he realized it was a terrible hypocrisy.

"I may convince others that communism works but I just can't convince myself. In fact, I don't believe a word of it! Property taken from the rich is not used to help the poor. The majority of Vietnamese are poor and all the government wants is to appeal to them and control them."

Nam discovered he was able to discuss his political views with his mother.

"It's good we were only middle class and not rich," Nam's mother stated in one conversation. "This way it may be a while yet until our house is confiscated. We can be thankful we never had a farm too."

"I know," Nam agreed. "If our government really used the property they take to help the poor it wouldn't be so bad but they give it to the political leaders from North Vietnam!"

The Vietnamese of the South, used to modern technology introduced by the long American presence in their country, found it particularly humiliating to be mastered by the Vietnamese of the North whom they considered less sophisicated, uncivilized and ignorant.

"Those Northerners drive confiscated Mercedes in shorts with their bare feet hanging out," Mrs. Tran scoffed. "And do you know that couple that moved into that mansion on the next street? They didn't know what a flush toilet was for. They decided it was a device for washing rice. So they washed their rice and when it all flushed away they figured it was the American way of cooking rice."

"Really?" Nam laughed hilariously.

"That's right," Mrs. Tran chuckled. "Of course they wouldn't admit their ignorance though. Northerners try to act so smart. They told their neighbors about it, making fun of the

Americans. 'Look how Americans cook their rice. What a foolish invention!' they said. When the neighbors explained what the flush toilet was for, those Northerners walked home in shame."

"I hear that many of them don't know what televisions and stereos are either," Nam added. "You may ask them if they have TVs and stereos in North Vietnam and they say, 'Yes, they're running all over the street! Seems like they're still living with nineteenth-century technology up there. Here they have to hire our people to show them how to operate equipment they're stealing from us!"

"And do you know what they call an automatic calendar watch, Mother?" Nam asked, greatly enjoying himself. "They call it an 'unman' with two windows. Anything automatic is too sophisticated for them. They can't figure it out."

"Communism is the most materialistic philosophy I know," Mrs. Tran commented quite seriously. "How much do they really own due to their own production? And, did they bring civilization to the South as they claim or did the south save the North?"

"My biggest question is," Nam asked, "How did they win the war? Was it material technology or was it their people's will, determination and propaganda? To me it seems that they're down to the 'lesser of two evils' philosophy, the notion of doing something wrong so things won't get worse. They'll take away a family member trying to shape up the whole family which in turn will shape up the whole country."

"How true," Nam's mother said thoughtfully. "You know, I can see five steps which they have been using to gain psychological and political control over society.

"First, they take everything from the rich and allow no private enterprise. The second step is control over the food supplies market. They dictate how many groceries each family can buy each week. That's one reason why they come to check every month how many people are in each household. This gets them to the third step where they make it impossible for people to produce their own supplies because the property belongs to the government. Thus they become dependent on the government.

"Fourthly, they know that a mother will do anything to feed her family. In making the family suffer hunger communism manipulates adults into doing almost anything they are told to do. Once the government has this much control the people have no choice but to join the labor camps and be drafted. That's the final step. They tell the workers they're being paid for that work but it's never enough to satisfactorily feed and clothe a family."

"Oh Mother," Nam declared passionately, "that's exactly how it is! How depressing and hopeless it sounds. We're locked in a groove and there's no way out. And to top it off they try to control even our daily routine.

"Every morning at six o'clock they broadcast the public announcements, full blast, on every street corner. Nobody needs an alarm clock anymore. We're told to get on to the street and exercise for half an hour. They boast that this will make us stronger. Of course they always make sure that at least one person from each household gets out on the street to pick up garbage, sweep the sidewalk or anything else for the city. They want to keep us busy so we won't have time to think and ask questions."

Mrs. Tran added, "And they manipulate us all day. From six-thirty to nine they bombard us with communist propaganda and music, trying to convince us that communism has improved our country. Soon we'll be a famous and powerful country! Finally at ten they turn down the volume so there's a little quietness but then they start door-to-door visitations to record what everyone is doing and where everyone is."

"They even tell us when we can go grocery shopping," Nam inserted.

"That's right! If we're lucky we can go once a week. Sometimes we have to wait two weeks before there are enough market supplies. And woe is me if I forget to take my shopping diary in which they can check that I won't buy more than our share. The other day I didn't go immediately after the announcement and I ended up waiting in line for eight hours! Eight hours — I wondered if it was worth the two cabbages and the kilo of rice I finally got! We're supposed to feel grateful if we get a dozen eggs occasionally or two bottles of 'luxury' watered-down pop."

"I know all about these disappointments," Nam said solicitiously. "I saw many desperate eyes and destitute faces when I served as a volunteer in the food markets. In fact I've learned a lot about the communist philosophy and way of life in the last few months. You know why I decided to accept re-education. . . . I should be indoctrinated enough now to get a job. It will make life a little easier for us. Next week I'll start applying for work again."

Nam tried unsuccessfully for two weeks. "Everytime I've almost convinced the employer to hire me they ask about my father's occupation. As soon as they find out that he's in a re-education camp for serving in the American army they strike my name off the list," Nam explained to Mrs. Tran.

"The only way I'd have a chance was if I had been born into a communist family or if I'd kill my father or if I became a communist informer reporting any anti-communist behavior and attitudes! Yes, all depends on one's background. Father's considered a criminal and I'm a social outcast."

When by September of 1976 Nam still had not found a job he decided to return to school. At least he would please his father.

With his former classmates now in grade twelve, however, and Nam repeating grade eleven, he felt greatly inferior. "Somehow I always managed to make a fool of myself in my attempts to make headway," he thought. He could not overcome his restlessness and sense of inferiority and once more he dropped out of school after a few months.

He then found private instructors and took a six-month mechanical course, then a few months of typing classes and then a course on fixing electrical appliances. He never obtained a certificate in any of the courses. For various reasons he always dropped out before he had completed it. Occasionally, between switching courses, he managed to find a few odd jobs.

6

"I HAVE SOMEONE TO LIVE FOR"

Once more Nam decided to return to the country. He found a job on a farm close to where his grandfather had lived. He worked on a field of sweet potatoes which was tended by hand. He enjoyed the outdoor labor and thought he might like to operate a farm of his own someday.

Ten days later Nam received pleasant news. His uncle, who had once lived in France, had permission to return to that country.

"I have to leave this job and return to Saigon to bid my uncle farewell," Nam told his boss.

"This revives my hope," Nam said to his uncle. "If you can return perhaps Mother can renew her French citizenship which she lost in the sixties and we might be able to leave someday too. She gave up her French citizenship when she married, but would you please do us the favor of investigating the possibilities of renewing her papers?" Nam pleaded.

"Yes Nam, I'll do whatever I can. I'm truly grateful that I can leave Vietnam and I'll do anything I can to help your family," his uncle promised.

Later Nam sat on the balcony, meditating. "Well I'm back at square one. I let the farming job go. My father is still in prison. I'm getting more tired every day of being driven by poverty and communist restrictions. Survival . . . even sticking to a job for any length of time calls for more creativity than I can manage. . . . Is there any answer to life's questions under this system? If there is, why can't I find it?"

Life seemed as dismal as the dark overcast sky. Nam pushed his hands into his pockets. He felt some cigarettes his farm boss had given him. He had never smoked, but it seemed as if it might be interesting. Perhaps it would ease his boredom. He lit a cigarette, smoked a few puffs and eased back in his chair.

At that moment Nam caught sight of Duyen, a girl from the neighborhood he had become acquainted with through the communist youth club.

"I sure seem to be seeing her a lot lately," Nam recalled. "Or is it just because I'm starting to notice her?"

Duyen was an outgoing and popular person. When they had first met Nam did not like her; in his opinion she was too assertive for a a girl. He knew that she was intelligent but her confident poise somehow irritated him.

Now Nam admitted to himself that he felt attracted to her and wanted to get to know her better. He knew that her mother had died soon after Duyen reached school age. Her father, too, was in prison.

"Life must be difficult for her," Nam realized. "I know what it's like to struggle through life unable to succeed. She always appears to be in control of the situation but maybe I've judged her too quickly. Maybe she's struggling just like I am." He wished he could talk to her.

But he had to find another job.

Nam hopped on his bike and cycled into the country for a couple of days without eating. Ostensibly he was looking for work but it was also part of his continuous search for freedom from oppression.

"It seems like each day makes me more miserable. I feel so alone, but there's no one with whom I can share my feelings," he complained to himself. "I wonder if anyone else ever feels tied up like I do under this system? I don't even know who I can trust with my feelings. If I say too much I could get caught and be imprisoned for . . . for who knows how long.

"Just the same," Nam thought, "I have to find someone with whom I can share my feelings and sorrow."

When Nam returned to Saigon he found a stack of his father's writing paper. Carefully he cut it into smaller pieces and stapled them together, making small notebooks. He took a handful and stepped on to the street to sell them.

"Hi Nam," Duyen said, passing by. "What are you doing now?"

"Uh, just selling notebooks," Nam said, forcing himself to be calm and keep the encounter business-like.

"May I see one?" Duyen reached out and took a notebook. "This is just what I need. Could I buy one?"

"Sure. That's what they're for." Nam sold her a notebook and hurried along.

Three days later Duyen strolled by while Nam worked on his bicycle. "Hello there," she called. "How's the salesman doing today?"

"Hi!" Nam said casually. "I've sold my notebooks. Maybe I can sell you a bike!"

"I have a bike but it doesn't work properly," the girl replied. "The chain keeps slipping off. I know you used to assemble used bicycles for trading. Would you mind taking a look at my bike? Perhaps you can repair it for me."

"Sure, I'll look at it right away."

Duyen carefully watched Nam as he repaired the bicycle.

"There, that should do it, Duyen," he said when he finished. "Do you want to give it a try? Let's go for a ride."

"You did a great job, Nam," Duyen complimented when they returned. "Thanks a lot."

During the next weeks Nam and Duyen cycled together some more.

"I think you're falling in love with that girl," Mrs. Tran teased when Nam returned late for supper one day.

"No way, Mother!" Nam responded quickly. "She's a

great gal all right, but we're just friends. I've got nothing else to do and we both love biking. I'm much too young to get serious about any girl."

But almost against Nam's will his love for Duyen grew. He got to know her better with each hour they spent together.

"Duyen, I feel that I've missed a lot by ignoring you all these years," Nam confessed. "I don't even know your family. You have only one brother, right? He's the oldest in the family?"

"You are both wrong and right," Duyen said playfully, looking into Nam's eyes for a quick second. "Yes, I have only one brother; but no, I'm the oldest. And then I also have two younger sisters."

"That explains a few things," Nam said. "That means with both of your parents gone you're like the head of your household. You must be a strong person to handle that responsibility."

"When you have no choice, you do what you have to do," Duyen stated. "It hasn't always been easy. Many times I feel weak, confused and helpless, but I have to put on a brave front for my younger siblings. They need me. They have no one else."

Spending time with Duyen helped Nam understand her. He realized why she was so well-liked by others. She was extraordinarily outgoing and confident, but at the same time she showed appreciation for others and encouraged them. Nam recognized that he was learning to love Duyen. He also knew that there were other young men who liked to be with her.

He could scarcely believe it when she accepted his invitation to a movie. "I'm competing against other guys who always seem to be more successful with everything than I am," Nam thought, reflecting on the evening. "I can't see why Duyen would have preferred my company to that of any of the others. She must have sensed my sincerity. She also enjoyed that part of the movie where the main character fought against the government. Perhaps Duyen and I have a lot more in common than I know. . . ."

Nam frequently went to Duyen's place after she returned from school to help her with her homework.

"I have so much difficulty with my English. I'm grateful that I found someone who can help me," Duyen said, smiling appreciatively.

"No problem, Duyen," Nam laughed. "Helping you with your homework sure beats sitting in class myself! By the way, do you need any more plants for your botany class?"

"Yes, I do. Would you have time to collect a few more samples for me?"

"There's nothing else to do," Nam answered. "Just tell me what you want and I'll try to collect them either here in the city or in the country."

Duyen searched her notes for an illustrated list of what she needed. "Here it is . . . I need leaves of these six plants. If you can find them for me I'll. . . ."

"You'll what?" Nam interrupted.

"I don't know," Duyen blushed. "I can't pay you because I have no extra money. What can I do to thank you for all the help you've been to me?"

"How about joining me for another forty-five kilometer ride in the country this weekend?"

"Sounds great!" Duyen's dark eyes glistened with delight.

On the morning of their outing a cool breeze ruffled their hair as they pedalled happily along a country road. When they reached their destination Duyen jumped off her bike and raced towards the river bank. Nam chased after her and grabbed her arm. "Are you trying to run away from me?" he teased.

"Yes!" she cried, laughing. "This fresh air and being away from the city does wonders for me. I feel so young and free away from the cares of my family." She continued to run along the river bank with Nam at her side.

After a while they stopped, sat down on a rock and quietly watched the river current. "The water looks so peaceful," Nam broke the silence. "In fact, all of nature — the wild flowers, grass, insects and birds — all of it speaks of peace and joy. Nature has nothing to worry about. I wish my life could be more peaceful, like nature is."

"What's your greatest worry, Nam?" Duyen asked softly.

"My greatest concern is knowing how to live under the communist regime. I've tried everything I can think of but it always ends in failure. Before I discovered you I felt I had nothing to live for."

"You mean I've actually made a difference to you?" Duyen looked at him questioningly.

"You certainly have," Nam assured her. "Life seems worthwhile again. On days when I don't see you I almost go crazy, missing you." Nam reached for Duyen's hand and gave it a light squeeze.

Duyen pondered his words for a while and then said, "Getting to know you better has changed my opinion of you. I used to think that you were proud. When you talked you sounded like you knew it all — and you looked so old and skinny! Now I've learned that you can be a lot of fun. You've been a tremendous support to me when I'm tired of being the head of the household."

"So that's what you thought of me? Smart-acting but dumb-looking?" Nam asked, chuckling. "Do you know what I thought of you? I thought you were aggressive, not feminine enough. I know now that you needed to put up a bold front. Do you know that you've also changed since we discovered each other."

"Have I really?"

"Yes, you have," Nam answered, his eyes searching Duyen's face. "You're not as bossy as you used to be . . . that is, as I used to think you were."

"It's probably because I've learned to put my trust in you," Duyen answered. "I've become very dependent on you for moral support. Somehow I'm not as worried about my family's well-being as I was."

"Duyen, I feel that we love each other very much. This country doesn't offer us much to live for but at least we have each other."

Nam paused for a few moments. He fumbled with pebbles in his hands. "I have nothing to offer you in terms of finances but I have a heart full of love for you," he said. "Duyen, do you think you could accept me as I am and become my wife?" Nam breathed a sigh of relief that he had finally asked her.

Duyen stared at the river for a long while. (To Nam it seemed an eternity!) Finally she straightened her back and cleared her throat.

"My love for you," she said, pausing to look at him evenly, "yes, it is deep. I love you enough to commit my life to you. As for your financial situation, I know how you've tried to earn a living. You've proved yourself to me by all you've struggled through.

"But," Duyen continued, turning to gaze at the river, "we're too young to get married. I have my family to take care of. My father is counting on me to do that."

"How long will your father expect you to stay at home? Doesn't he ever think of re-marrying?" Nam asked.

"I have no idea how long he'll be in prison. Until he can return I'm in charge at home. As for his re-marrying, well, he always says that too many stepmothers turn out to be a curse on the family. He doesn't want that to happen to us," Duyen explained.

"Duyen, if we married you could still live with your family," Nam said. "I know that traditionally the bride moves in with the groom's family but we live so close together it shouldn't make that much difference. I wouldn't have a problem spending most of our time with your family. Let's see what our parents think about it."

Mrs. Tran was shocked when Nam informed her that he planned to marry. "Judging by the amount of time you spend with Duyen I should have known it was coming. But you're only eighteen! You're much too young to get married. You have no means of supporting a wife."

"I know that Mother, but I love her. I can't stand living without her any longer. She gives me new hope and purpose. I have someone to share my feelings with. Who knows, I may soon be drafted into the labor force or be killed one way or the other. If I marry, I may be lucky to have a son. He will carry on the family name. Maybe that will be the only noteworthy contribution I'll ever make toward our family."

In the meantime Nam and Duyen kept on seeing each other. They discussed their beliefs. Duyen's family was traditionally Buddhist while Nam's family was Catholic. In discussing their religious differences Nam told Duyen that Jesus was the focus of his life rather that Buddha. "Would you be willing to give up Buddhism and become a Catholic?" Nam questioned.

"It doesn't make any difference to me," Duyen stated. "I've never felt very strongly for Buddhism. I see no problem with our differing religious backgrounds."

Nam continued to pursue the possibility of their marriage. Finally his parents and Duyen's father consented in spite of the criticisms of many friends and neighbors.

The small family wedding was celebrated at the Tran house on November 17, 1977. Nam spoke to the guests.

"This is a celebration of our love for each other. We didn't have the money to prepare a banquet; we aren't even taking pictures. All we have to offer is tea and cookies. But what matters most is that we have love. Now I have someone to live for. I don't know how long we'll be able to stay together but today is all that matters. Today I have Duyen and she has me.

"In the past I underestimated Duyen's bravery, her abilities and determination. I've discovered that she learned very early in life to handle large responsibilities. Now we fill the gaps for each other. Where one of us is weak and lacks courage the other is strong. We feel we were made for each other."

Mrs. Tran reflected on how traditions had changed over the years. "It used to be that weddings were sad occasions for the bride. The marriage was pre-arranged by the parents and often the bride scarcely knew the groom. She had to leave her family and move in with a strange family.

"This is not the case with Nam and Duyen. Their relationship is based on love and has had a chance to develop over a period of time. I am pleased to accept Duyen into our family and have her move in with us!"

The ceremony of love ended with Nam and Duyen signing their marriage application. It was signed by two witnesses and a few days later Nam presented the application at City Hall to be registered and signed.

Duyen moved in with the Tran family but continued to spend much of her time in her father's household ensuring that the domestic matters were properly looked after.

Nam's next concern was to become the father of a son so as to fulfill his role in continuing the family name. This responsibility would naturally bring with it a greater need for a satisfactory job to provide for his family.

The price of government rice in Saigon was extremely high and the quality was poor. It had been donated by other countries during the war. Often people ate barley, imported from Russia, rather than this unpalatable rice.

Nam moved some 160 kilometers south to the rice-growing region, the richest part of the country. From there he smuggled twenty-five kilo bags of fresh rice into the city.

His only means of transportation back and forth was on old, badly crowded buses or on the backs of trucks. He had to pass through numerous check stations. Smuggling was very risky. Nam soon figured out a method of producing his own permit under the pretense of being someone else.

Usually he left the country between nine and ten at night and arrived in Saigon by three or four in the morning. Then he spent several hours at home before proceeding to sell the rice. As before, however, this enterprise lasted only a few weeks.

7

"WHAT ABOUT ESCAPING?"

In the spring of 1978, Nam found himself getting restless again. With both Nam's and Duyen's fathers still in prison survival for the family became more critical. Nam also knew that at any time he could be drafted by the army or labor team. Since Mr. Tran had worked for the previous regime Nam realized he would be disqualified for army service, so it was almost certain that he would have to join a labor team and work without wages.

The labor teams were a government plan whereby people could be called up to work at any time. They could be sent to any location in Vietnam and received barely enough to feed themselves while the profits were channelled into the government treasury. Nam knew this would make life for his family even more difficult and wondered if there was any way of avoiding the labor team.

In October, 1978, Duyen gave birth to their first child. "It's a boy!" she cried joyfully. "Oh Nam, I'm so excited. Our dream has come true." Duyen found much pleasure in caring for baby Bao.

Nam was thrilled but he was also very much aware that his responsibilities as the breadwinner had just become more demanding.

A few days later Nam received the dreaded first call from the labor team. He ignored it. After the second call, unable to find an excuse, he registered. He was sent to an area some thirty kilometers from Saigon. The project was disorganized and Nam found the government attempt to control others' lives disgusting.

"My family is at home worrying about me. They're left without support. And I'm here in this uncivilized place, bombarded with communist propaganda and forced to do things I never planned to do. I've got to get out of here."

Nam ran away from the camp. He rationalized that his absence would not be noticed for several days because the camp was so disorganized.

Fearful of being discovered, however, Nam quickly and cautiously walked the two kilometers to the nearest public transportation, a water taxi. Reaching the river he learned that he would have to wait until enough passengers came to fill the boat. Nam tried to keep as calm as possible, silently praying, "God don't let me get caught. I so desperately long to see Duyen and Bao. Please don't let anything hinder me from returning home safely."

Several hours on the water taxi brought Nam to the center of Saigon where he caught a ride on the outside of a bus. With one foot on the step and his hands tightly holding the railing he finally reached his home late in the evening.

A month later Nam received notice that if he did not return to the labor camp he would be punished. Nam promptly took to the streets, living a fugitive life, dropping in at home only occasionally to see how his family was keeping.

"I can't support my family physically or financially but at least I can try to help them emotionally," he often consoled himself.

Bao was now old enough to stay with Mrs. Tran, so Duyen went to work. Her salary barely provided food for herself and her son.

"I can't give up. My family needs me, but . . . I can't even support myself. There's got to be a way out of this dilemma."

Nam clenched his fists in bitterness.

Like a wild beast chased by a hunter, Nam fled from one friend's home to another, taking care not to endanger his hosts should he be located.

One day Nam met a former classmate. They began to discuss politics and soon discovered that they had many opinions in common. They decided to meet at a friend's house later to continue their discussion.

Because Nam had studied mechanics his friend asked, "What other skills do you have? Would you be interested in joining an underground group against the government? Or, what about escaping the country?"

"I've never considered that," Nam answered slowly. "I've always been taught to be loyal to my country, to strive to make it a better place to live. I've heard of people escaping, but then I ask myself, what if the other country is no better? What would I do then, escape again?"

Nam's friend continued to urge Nam to try escaping.

"I'll think it over," Nam finally agreed. "But give me some time. It all seems rather risky to me."

The option of leaving illegally led to another series of sleepless nights.

"My family's financial situation is enough reason to leave," he argued inwardly, "but my conscience troubles me. Leaving means that I've been defeated and can't help my country the way I would like. Deep down I keep hoping things will change for the better in Vietnam. Sooner or later, though, I'll be drafted for the labor camp again. Many die there due to poor nutrition. Here in Vietnam my future can only get worse. . . ."

His family was in financial need. Every time Nam returned home the picture became more depressing. All eyes communicated worries about their next meal. Occasionally they sold a shirt on the black market to buy food for the day.

"I have to do something to help them," Nam lamented.

He reached a decision: he would proceed with plans to escape.

When Nam discussed it with his family, Mrs. Tran encouraged him. "I think it would be a wise move," she said. "It might be your only chance. Perhaps you can free the rest of the family eventually if you escape now."

Duyen was more hesitant. "Nam, I need you. I don't want you to leave." She burst into tears.

Nam placed his strong arms around her and held her tightly. "This isn't my decision. This isn't what I want. Duty calls me to leave. This may be the only way we can have a meaningful life together as a family."

"What if something happens . . . you drown, or . . ." Sobbing, Duyen clung to Nam.

"I'd like to promise you that we'll meet again, Duyen. I can't be sure, but I still think it's worth the risk."

Nam realized that Duyen had changed since he first met her. "She used to be so independent," he thought. "Now that we're married she has become dependent on me. Dare I let her down? She desperately needs my emotional support even though I've failed to provide for her financially."

"Why should I be the one to suffer all the time?" Duyen grieved. "My mother died, and then my father was taken captive. I've hurt and suffered loneliness until I felt I couldn't stand it any longer. I found happiness in you when I desperately needed someone. I've learned to put my trust in you and to lean on you. Now you want to leave. Why do I always have to be the one to get hurt?" Duyen's eyes were swollen from crying and Nam's shirt was soaked with her tears.

One day Nam's friend contacted him. "The trip is all planned. You have to take a brief orientation and you'll be the sailor or mechanical assistant," he advised him.

That night Nam told Duyen about his final plans. "Duyen, I have no choice but to make this attempt. I hope I'll be able to make your future brighter this way.

"Mother promised to continue caring for Bao so that you can keep your job at the sewing factory. I'll contact you as soon as I've made a safe escape."

"Nam, I hate to see you go. I'm going to miss you but I realize that Vietnam has nothing to offer you. I'll pray that you escape safely." As much as she opposed his departure, Duyen knew she would not be able to convince him to change his mind. She tried to suppress her emotions; weeping now would only make it more difficult for him.

With a heavy heart, Nam bid his wife farewell and made his way to the riverside. "I hate to leave my family, not knowing whether I'll ever meet them again," he thought, "but . . . I have a feeling that I'll get caught and soon be back — in the same old rut — again."

The fourteen by five meter boat was in excellent condition. All six crew members were excited and their departure went smoothly. The left on the river near the city center during the daytime, at the right time of the tide to sail smoothly from the river into the sea. They hoped to reach the mouth of the river just before sunset. "By the time we reach the sea, darkness will help hide us from the guards," the captain explained.

Slowly and cautiously they approached the check station they would need to clear in order to continue. Nam's heart pounded rapidly. He sensed a mood of anxiety among all the men. Everyone's muscles were taut.

Nam noticed one of the older men taking charge and giving orders. "He must have been in a situation like this before," Nam whispered to Tuan, his close friend. "I'm glad someone knows what to do."

Nam experienced a strange numbness. "My arms feel as if they're not a part of me anymore; they're just trembling on their own. I have to calm them down somehow. Why am I so afraid? I'll try to act normally and I'm sure everything will be just fine."

Nam forced himself to get to his feet. All his muscles were tense; his hands and feet were perspiring. He followed the captain's order and came forward.

Pretending to be an experienced sailor Nam awkwardly loosened the anchor rope. He made himself smile broadly.

Some twenty meters from the station Nam began to shake and a cold shiver rippled down his spine. "Oh God! I'm going to die." Nam clung to the rope. "I can't handle this. I'm going to faint. Oh God, please help us through. I'm doing this for my family, not for myself. You've got to help us. Please protect us."

Nam became progessively more terrified as they neared the station. "What will the guards do when they find out we're escaping Vietnam?" Nam worried, his fingernails digging into his clenched fists.

"Oh, I don't want to think about it! I'll be imprisoned. My family will die when they hear it. They placed all their hope in me. My friends are counting on me too. If I get caught how will I ever be able to go free again?

"Oh God, please help us," Nam turned his pleading face upward. "We're helpless right now. Show us your miraculous power."

Suddenly Nam regained confidence and strength. He felt God's answer to his cry. He was sure that God would guide them through this dilemma.

"I'm the greatest coward there is, yet I've always acted like I was brave and determined and unbeatable. I've lived a lie!" It was a startling insight.

The boat finally arrived at the check station and stopped. A soldier boarded and thoroughly checked every part of the boat.

Two more soldiers came on board. They too investigated every nook and corner.

"What's behind that board?" A soldier pointed to a section in the wall that obviously had been removed at one point.

"I don't know," the captain tried to answer calmly.

The officer grabbed a crowbar and wrenched off the board. The six members of the crew exchanged quick, horrified glances, "How will we explain this?" each one wondered.

The officer recklessly pulled out piles of women's and children's clothing and threw them on the floor. "What does this mean?" he stormed. "You said you didn't know what was in here."

The soldier stared at the men, waiting for an answer. No one dared speak. The clothes belonged to people waiting at various locations along the river who would be picked up later that evening. Nobody wanted to reveal the truth so all decided to let the captain do the talking.

"I don't know who these clothes belong to," the captain said, appearing baffled. "I didn't know they were in here. They must belong to the previous owner of this boat."

The soldiers suspected that the captain and his men were attempting escape. Since they couldn't prove it, however, they took the boat into custody. The men were ordered to stay on the vessel all night.

Once the soldiers left them the men huddled for a conference. "They're not convinced that we're innocent," the captain stated. "They'll ask us more questions tomorrow. I'm sure they'll check our fuel barrels too. When they discover eight hundred liters of diesel fuel they'll suspect us still more. We have to get rid of the fuel. We have no choice but to drain it into the river. But I tell you, it has to be done quietly!"

That night four of the men formed an assembly line for the task on hand. The first man filled a bucket and passed it on. The fourth man quietly poured it into the river. The moving stream carried the fuel silently away into the sea. By dawn the barrels were empty and there was no trace of diesel fuel left.

In the morning another soldier came to make further investigations. He seemed sympathetic to the men, as if doing his inspection duty out of obligation. He promised to do all he could to set the six men free.

"By the way, one of the soldiers at this station is sick and we're running low on groceries. Could we buy one of your ducks for today's supper?" the soldier inquired.

"Certainly," the captain replied. "Here, you can take this one."

Later the soldier returned. "I noticed you have a cassette

radio. May we borrow it just for tonight?"

"Yes," said the captain, handing him the radio.

"I know what he's doing," Nam said indignantly after the soldier left. "He speaks politely but in reality he's just stealing our property. He knows he has control over us and he knows that we know if we'd refuse him these articles we'd be in trouble. He's pretending to be kind so that we won't catch on to his tactics."

Sure enough, later that day he returned to request the guitar and some rice. Both times the captain consented.

"This is crazy," muttered the captain. "But if I refuse we have no chance at all of being released."

By the evening the only food left was one duck. The men cooked it and ate their supper.

"Wonder what we'll do tomorrow?" Tuan sighed.

"I sure don't know," replied the captain. "They've stolen just about all our belongings so there's not much point in keeping us here any longer."

"Why don't we quietly swim away tonight?" Nam suggested.

"No way," Tuan stated. "This boat belongs to my family. We can't just leave it. That would be too big a loss."

Nam did some quick mental calculating and realized that leaving the ship would mean a loss of some thirty thousand dollars. "I guess you're right, Tuan. Well then, we'll just have to wait it out and see what happens."

The next day the men attempted to hide their anxiety by playing chess and napping. In the late afternoon they noticed a taxi boat at the check station.

"That's the soldier that promised to help free us." Tuan pointed to the soldier stepping off the taxi boat. "He looks different today. Not nearly as official as he did yesterday."

"Maybe he has a different role today," Nam said. "Look. Isn't he heading in our direction now?"

"Sure is," the captain observed. "I hope he has good news."

Once more the soldier came on board. "Were you planning to escape?" he questioned the captain.

"No," lied the captain. "We were just going for a ride on the river. We wouldn't dream of trying to escape Vietnam. It's a big mistake that we are being held like this."

"All right. If that's true give me all your gold and you may return to Saigon this evening," the soldier ordered.

The men gave him what gold they had and turned the boat in the direction of the city.

"Well, we have a lot to be thankful for," Nam reminded the others on their trip back. "At least we weren't imprisoned or killed. This experience hasn't been all that bad after all. I lacked confidence at the start but now that I have some practice I'd like to try an escape another time."

"Me too," Tuan agreed. "I still have the boat. I'm not giving up now! I'll start planning again as soon as I get home. Are you ready to join me in planning another escape, Nam?"

"I sure am," Nam said firmly. "Let's try again."

8

"IF WE CAN ONLY GET TO SEA . . ."

The same group of men re-organized and attempted another escape several weeks later. This time Nam, with three passengers, left the city center two hours before sunset. Other passengers were picked up at various locations along the river.

"We're approaching the station where we got caught last time," Nam whispered to his companions. "If we can only make it past that station somehow we might be safe."

"The large boat ahead of us is a licensed boat which doesn't need to stop to report. If you can keep this boat on the left side of it we may be lucky enough to sneak by," Nam's comrade advised.

After a half-hour of near breath-holding silence Nam gasped out to the others, "We did it! We're past! I can't believe it!"

From there they chugged into a small river, taking them to a bigger river. Never in his life had Nam seen such a wide river. By this time it was completely dark and the thought of traversing such a gigantic waterway sent shivers of fear through the boat's occupants, most of them completely inexperienced in the ways of water travel.

"I've never even been on the sea before, never mind being an amateur sailor," Nam thought. "And I've got all this responsibility for our passengers. How will I do it?"

The boat continued along the river as previously arranged. The man who would be their captain was the last on the list to be picked up. When they reached the designated spot, however, he was not there. No one knew his whereabouts.

"I hope he comes soon," Nam worried. "If he doesn't show up soon we'll just have to leave without him."

"How can we manage without him?" questioned one of the passengers. "After all, he arranged everything and he knows the river currents and possible dangers better than any of us."

"I know," Nam admitted. "We need him badly! Still I'd sooner give it a try than wait here and get caught. I think we could get away on our own but what worries me in travelling without a captain is, what if something goes wrong with the boat?"

The group of about fifty people waited tensely on the river bank. One hour, and then two, passed by.

"The longer we wait, the more anxious I get," Tuan said. "We can't afford to give up now and go back home. But if we leave on our own we may not make it safely. Where in the world can he be staying?"

"Let's leave without him," Nam suggested.

The rest of the company agreed and boarded the boat. They appointed a committee of men to take the place of a captain.

Once they were into the river Nam realized their delay made the present situation dangerous. "Because we left two hours later than we had planned, we're running against tide," he confided to several others. "This will slow us down even more. We wanted to be out of the river and well out at sea before sunrise. At this rate, though, we'll never get out by morning."

The captains propelled the boat against tide as fast and as calmly as they possibly could. Every muscle in their bodies strained, taut with exertion and frustration. His fists clenched, Nam peered desperately ahead into the dark sea, as if to somehow make the boat move faster.

"We've got to make it," he told himself. "If we can only get to sea by daybreak it could mean freedom. Freedom! Is it possible? Oh, we've got to keep pushing. We can't afford to slow down one bit."

Each minute of their journey increased Nam's nervousness. "We're getting close to the mouth of the river," he realized. He felt like shouting it.

"I'd better keep quiet," he reminded himself. "We never know where secret policemen are staged. Oh God, please let us get away safely. I feel like we're so close to reaching freedom at last."

After several hours of travel Nam began to relax. He felt confident now that the men in charge would bring them to safety. They were older and more experienced than he was. He dared to close his eyes for a moment and just as soon, he fell asleep. He slept for several hours.

Gun shots awakened him at the break of dawn.

"Oh no!" he groaned in terror. There were boats chasing them. They must be boats of the secret police!

The women screamed. The children cried out too, not understanding what was happening. The men weere suddenly hysterical. "Keep on going!" some shouted. "Speed up! We've got to get away."

Other voices pleaded for the captains to stop. "Let's try to settle it before we're all killed," they argued.

One man removed his white shirt and waved it in the air as a sign of surrender. It made no difference to their pursuers. They did not stop shooting.

Nam shouted encouragement to the leaders. "Just keep giving it all you have! Our boat is in excellent condition. All that can happen is some bullet holes in our boat. We have enough people along to dip out water if we get a few leaks."

"No, let's stop," the older men argued. "We must consider the women and children. They'll perish of fear. We have to stop for their sakes."

The captains halted the boat. The enemy continued to

charge forward, and one of them smashed into the side of the refugee vessel, almost breaking it. A man sitting on that side was hit in the collision. His head slashed open. Blood squirted over his face from a deep slash on his head.

The policemen rushed on deck. "They're crazier than animals," Nam muttered, "the way they're pointing their guns at us."

Roughly, the policemen forced the males into one tiny room. They were cramped like fish in a tin and felt they would expire from sweat and lack of oxygen. The could hear more shooting on deck.

"We promise to release the men if you will hand over all your gold and money," the police announced to the women and children who huddled fearfully together.

Helpless and powerless, concerned above all for the safety of the men, the women unhesitatingly allowed their assailants whatever money and valuables they had. The policemen scurried about eagerly collecting everything that appealed to them.

Just when they were about to release the men a coast guard cutter chanced by the scene. The coast guards in their turn confiscated the gold and captured the refugees.

Now the escapees realized it was not policemen who had stopped them, but rather terrorist fishermen. Vietnamese pirates!

The coast guard cutter towed the refugee boat back to land. Then the men were handcuffed and all fifty passengers forced to walk several kilometers to the nearest county jail. Several army jeeps escorted them to the prison.

The dejected group crossed through a crowded marketplace. "Let them go!" shouted some shoppers sympathetically. Others stood still, staring, too shocked to speak.

One woman slyly kept to the outer edge of the prisoner caravan. With perfect timing she moved to a market seller and perched beside her. The guards never noticed her escape.

At the county jail everyone had to line up by families and each family was given a little water to drink and a small serving of rice.

Without family or relatives, Nam found himself alone. He was busily scheming. "How will I identify myself?" he debated. "I'll have to think up a story that will make me 'not guilty' of attempting to escape."

"I have no family," he told the first officer in the registration. "They have all died." Nam proceeded to relate tragic family experiences of the last five years. Several more officers interviewed him and each time he carefully explained that he was the only person in his family.

"I was on the boat because I have no family members left," he told them. "I believe in communism but was talked into escaping. In fact, when we left I didn't even know the others were planning to leave the country. When I realized what was happening it was too late to get off the boat."

Nam was among some forty men who were then quartered in a three by six meter room. The metal walls were lined with barbed wire and two small holes in one wall were their only source of ventilation.

At night the men lay body to body on the concrete floor. Nam wore only a pair of shorts and had no blanket. Part of his body ached from the cold concrete floor while the rest of him dripped sweat from the sweltering heat transmitted through the metal roof. Two older men beside him complained about homosexual activity at the other end of the room.

Nam couldn't sleep. He relived the day's events. In spite of the disappointing end of the escape attempt, he felt more determined than ever to leave Vietnam.

"As soon as I get out of here, I'm trying again," he promised himself. "Next time I'll leave with a smaller group. We won't have anybody over thirty. Those older men are too cautious. I'm leaving with young men who will dare to take a risk for freedom's sake."

In the morning everyone was allowed a once-a-day escorted trip to the washroom. Those who could not wait from one morning to the next received no consideration from the prison guards. The cell reeked accordingly.

"How can anyone be this merciless?" Nam wondered. "I never imagined jail this bad. Has my father gone through similar experiences?"

The second day the group was divided into smaller units and dispersed to various cells. Everyone went through another series of interviews by the jailers. Nam repeatedly stated that his family members were all dead, that he alone was alive.

When Nam entered his newly assigned cell he was shocked at what he saw. There were men who had been in prison for years but they seemed content and happy.

"I guess they have no choice," Nam concluded. "If they're not happy they'll just die that much sooner. They're taking a day at a time hoping for a better tomorrow. No prison sentence has been given, so they may be here for ten days or ten weeks, ten months, ten years, or for life — they don't know."

Nam found it difficult to understand these men, however. "Life out of prison is certainly better than this," he thought. "I'm realizing more and more all the time why people are willing to risk their lives for the sake of freedom."

After a few days Nam's group was separated and he was transferred to a larger provincial jail by boat. He had no idea where they were headed and most of his companions were strangers.

Although the prisoners had no clue as to where they were going or for how long, they welcomed the fresh air. For once they felt like breathing voluntarily. But they realized that their situation could get worse and were careful not to let briefly-improved treatment deceive them.

When they arrived at their destination everyone had to sit on the grass for a roll call. "What have you had to eat today?" called a prison guard.

"Nothing," shouted several men. "We haven't had anything to eat for several days."

"Well, what do you expect?" replied the guard indignantly.

Once more the men were assigned cells. This time Nam was placed in a cell about three times bigger than the previous one. He shared it with thirty to forty other men. One improvement was a wooden sleeping deck about two feet off the floor, but not everyone had room on it. Nam had to sleep on the concrete floor again, under the deck.

Nam did not know how long he would be in prison. His family had no idea where he was and yet it was their duty to supply him with food, clothing and personal belongings.

"With a temperature of 40° C. under this tin room I don't need much in the way of clothing," he thought, "but the food ration here is ridiculous. Not even a mouse could stay alive on it."

But at first Nam was too tired and depressed to eat even the limited food rations. All he did was think about his family and his future. There was little conversation in the cell. Everyone lay quietly with his own worries and feelings, afraid to express himself.

After a few days Nam adjusted somewhat to the daily routine. Each prisoner had to roll out his bedding and retire for the night at the same time. Some inmates were privileged to have family members who knew of their needs and brought them blankets as well as other personal belongings.

Nam had no bedding but he pulled on his only pair of pants and his jacket for the night. He did not even have a mosquito net like most other men did.

Lights were switched off at nine and no one was allowed to speak a word after that. The alarm sounded at five in the morning. Those men who had their own cups had set them in line the previous evening. In the morning the men rose according to the order of the cups and were escorted to the washroom.

Nam had no cup so he waited until someone else who was finished offered him the use of a cup. He usually ended up being the last one to the washroom. He had no toothbrush or toothpaste either but a friend gave him salt to rinse his mouth. Each prisoner was allowed only a liter of water per day for personal hygiene.

Nam was frequently dependent on the generosity of fellow inmates. He realized that his lie about family was a strike against him. "I dare not send a letter to my family now. If the officers ever find out I still have live family members I'll never make it out of here. But how can I notify them so they can bring me some supplies?" Nam worried.

For breakfast everyone put out a mug for boiling water which could be used for coffee, instant noodle soup, or whatever one had available. Once more Nam relied on the mercies of others.

After breakfast the prisoners exercised, closely monitored by the guards. Should anyone bump against the tin wall the noise alerted the guards, who were always suspicious that someone might attempt escape.

After ten in the morning the cell was quiet. Everyone napped or lay thinking. Tiny openings and nail holes in the tin roof allowed light to trickle in.

For lunch every man received a small dish of rice and several fish, each six to ten centimeters long. The supper menu was the same. "I never liked fish meat before, but I'm sure learning to appreciate it," Nam realized ruefully.

He recalled once reading that chewing food until it liquified gave it more nutritional value. He tried this, chewing each mouthful of rice until it was watery. He discovered that by doing this he did not feel hungry as quickly either. He lasted from meal to meal without the severe hunger pangs he had experienced before. He also determined, "I must learn not to let my stomach bother my mind."

A part of the daily schedule was the study and memorization of prison rules and regulations combined with times of singing. Nam was given a pair of plastic drums to play during these sessions. The rule was: "Sing as loudly as possible to cheer yourself up."

A number of prisoners owned chess games so Nam joined in many a chess combat during the long prison days. "If there's any benefit in my being in prison," he sometimes joked, "it's that I'm learning to play chess — and I have time to play it too!"

Nam learned much from an elderly inmate, who shared his life story with Nam. "I come from North Vietnam," he explained. "I used to be a rebel. When I was thirty I went to France and took a course in engineering. I learned that if I ever were to accomplish anything I'd have to fight for it. Life is a jungle and you have to fight to come through successfully."

"It's hard to believe that you were so aggressive, because you're so small," Nam commented. "You must have had a strong will. Listening to you talk about your experiences inspires me to be bold and courageous like you were."

Nam developed his own philosophy of life. "I have a strong mind and can control myself. I've learned to chew my rice so that I get sufficient nutrition. I may be in prison but I've been given brains to direct myself out of this environment. I can ignore myself physically. I know I'm skinny but I believe I'm still strong."

Whenever volunteers were needed to chop wood, Nam offered. It gave him a chance to be outside and breathe fresh air. Usually he found a few cherries; eating them was a luxurious experience.

Periodically two men were required to carry out the heavy barrels of garbage. One time when Nam attempted to lift the barrel he realized to his dismay that he was not as strong as he had thought he was. He collapsed. His partner made fun of Nam's weakness. Nam got up in shame and then they carried out the barrel together.

"This isn't fair," Nam grumbled. "His family brings him extra food. My family doesn't even know I'm here. I can't help it that I'm getting so weak."

During the first two months of his imprisonment Nam was thoroughly interrogated. The officers threatened, "If you won't tell us everything about yourself we'll put you in an isolated cell for twenty years. You'll get only one bowl of rice a day and be molested by mosquitos. Many prisoners die in isolation, you know."

Nam persistently claimed that all his family members were dead.

"I'm tired of this cross-examination," Nam thought in self-pity. "I know I'll be here for a long time. Physically I'm deteriorating rapidly. I'll have to send a message to my family soon, so they can send me some food. But how can I do that without revealing to the prison officers that I do indeed have family? The guards check all the letters we write. I have to send a message with an inmate's relatives very soon, but whom can I trust?"

Finally Nam sent a note to a distant cousin. In the letter he stated, "Take this message to your third aunt. Tell her I'm here and need supplies."

When Nam's cousin received the message he could make no sense out of it. He knew only Nam's nickname so did not even realize who had written the letter. He took it to his father. The older man quickly determined who the sender was but also found the message confusing.

"You have no third aunt," he told his son. "Or . . . wait a minute, your third uncle is Nam's father. Maybe that's what he means. Bring this letter to Nam's mother."

Nam realized the risk he had taken. "Maybe my cousin won't understand what I mean," he worried. "But if the message does get through to my family and one of them comes to visit me they'll have to report what connection we have. Then the officers will know I've lied . . . and then who knows what will happen to me?"

Nam attempted to keep as busy as possible. He volunteered at every opportunity to cut grass and chop wood, hoping the exercise would strengthen him and keep his mind occupied while he waited out the days of imprisonment.

9

"IT'S TIME TO SAY GOOD-BYE"

Duyen eventually received the message of Nam's imprisonment. Quickly she prepared a package with a change of clothing, a cup and bowl, a set of cutlery, a light blanket, dried noodles, soup mixes, tea, and vegetables for him.

When she arrived at the prison office the guard asked, "What is your relationship to Nam?"

"He's a close friend of mine," Duyen responded quickly. It was as if the words popped out of her mouth before she had realized what she said.

"Nam," called the prison guard. "I have some supplies for you."

Nam was overwhelmed to learn that his message had reached Duyen and that she had delivered two bags of provisions for him. He was not allowed to see her but he found a love note rolled up in a package of cigarettes.

Seeing the gifts renewed Nam's deep admiration for Duyen. "I can't believe she really did this," he thought. "First, I hardly expected her to get the message. Secondly, I didn't think she would find her way with the limited information I was able to give. She's so brave and intelligent."

Nam graciously shared his food supplies with several inmates who had become his friends.

The second time Duyen brought food her secret note in the cigarette box was discovered. When the officers read "The family is doing fine," they threatened not to deliver the goods. Duyen tactfully pleaded with them until they promised to pass them on.

Duyen longed to see Nam. She found it nearly unbearable to be so close to him and yet not have even a glimpse of him. But prison policy forbade any contact. She consoled herself that she knew where her husband was and that she could at least meet some of his needs.

Gradually living conditions in the prison improved. Nam became progressvely more anxious about the future, however.

One day when he was cleaning up the outside yard Nam noted that the previously stern and intimidating guard smiled at him. "It must be a sign of something," Nam thought. "I wonder if my release is actually getting closer?"

Several days later the prison cook whispered to Nam, "The guard is working on a list of people who will be released. I saw your name on the list. Don't you dare show that you know about it though or I'll be in trouble for telling you!"

Meanwhile Duyen prepared for a third trip to the prison. She held Bao in her arms as she tucked the last items into a bag. She stroked the toddler's hair and hugged him, whispering lest any spying neighbor should be listening, "Mommy's going to bring Daddy more food today. We haven't seen him for four months now, have we? Oh baby, you hardly know your father. But I do hope I'll be able to see him today."

Duyen left early, walking to a nearby bus stop. It was a five-hour ride and she wondered how many more times she would have to make the trip before Nam would be released. "Sometimes I think I can't take the uncertainty any longer," she thought, brushing away tears while pretending to be absorbed in the passing scenery.

"Nam has been trying so desperately to get ahead in life, but it seems he always meets a brick wall. I want him home with me so badly but I know that won't bring him peace and satisfaction either . . . but right now I'd give anything just to see him again."

At the prison camp Duyen stepped wearily into the office. A guard glared at her. "What do you want?" he snapped.

"I brought some food supplies for Nam Tran," she stated. "Please sir, could I talk to him?"

"No," he growled. He took the package and turned away.

Greatly disappointed, Duyen left the prison camp. Questions tumbled ceaselessly within her as she sat another five hours on the bus back to Saigon.

"I wonder how Nam is doing? Will he ever come home again? How does he feel? Will our living conditions ever improve? Dare I hope for a better future?

"God help him," she breathed a prayer.

Nam received the supplies from Duyen at three o'clock that afternoon. At five o'clock he was released from prison.

Before leaving he cheerfully presented his package to a miserably skinny cell-mate.

"If I ever get out of prison I'll look you up, Nam," the man said gratefully.

"You needn't try because you may not find me," Nam responded confidently.

With great anticipation Nam boarded the bus to travel home. "Boy, will Duyen be excited to see me! I wonder if I should burst into the house and surprise everyone or just walk in quietly, pretending nothing has happened? That way I may keep the neighbors from seeing too much."

At the bus station Nam happened to meet a former prison-mate. "Come to my house for a bowl of soup and we can chat for a while," he urged. "We have lots of experiences to share."

Nam searched his pocket for taxi fare. "I have just enough money to get to your place. That will bring me a little closer to home," he agreed.

The bowl of nutritious vegetable soup was delicious and satisfying, a wonderful way to begin his life out of prison. "Thank you," he said, "and I must hurry home now."

Nam walked several blocks to his relative Lan's house. Lan opened the door but stepped back when she saw him.

"W-what are you doing here?" she cried, concerned. "Where have you been?"

"I've been in jail," Nam answered. "I was released a couple of hours ago."

By now the sister of Lan's grandmother appeared at the door. "You're so pale, Nam. Have you been sick?" she inquired. "And your clothes, they're so dirty. What are you doing?" She feared he was involved in drugs.

"I was in prison until this afternoon," Nam repeated.

"Why aren't you going home then? Seems to me a man should attend to his own family before he calls on more distant relatives," the elderly lady scolded.

"Lan, could you please lend me your bike to go home?" Nam asked. "I don't have money for a taxi and it is going to be quite late if I walk all the way."

Lan was still not sure whether Nam was to be trusted. She had not seen him for almost half a year and in days like this one could never know whom to believe. "No, I won't lend you my bike," she said. "I'd rather lend you the money to pay your taxi fare."

Nam graciously accepted the money. On the one-block walk from the taxi stop to his home numerous neighbors noticed him and questioned him. "We thought you had left the country," they said. "How come you look so pale? Where have you been?"

Nam realized he would have to answer with care in order to protect his family. At first he tried to ignore them. The neighbors refused to accept the rebuff so Nam said, "I worked down south and caught malaria. I've been hospitalized for a couple of months. That's why I'm so pale and skinny."

The answer aroused their sympathy and stopped their queries.

Unsure where Duyen would be, Nam walked to his parents' house. He opened the door and said casually, "Good evening, Mother."

"Nam!" Mrs. Tran shrieked. She dropped her sewing and sprang up.

Nam laughed. "I've never seen you jump for joy before, Mother. And that with tears rolling down your cheeks."

"I'm so relieved to see you, Nam. We were so worried about you. You should have seen Duyen tonight. She was totally exhausted and depressed when she came back a few hours ago."

By now Nam's four sisters and six-year-old brother Jean had surrounded him, jumping and shouting for joy at seeing him again.

"Where's Duyen?" Nam asked. "I have to see her before I answer your questions."

"She's at her father's house. Jean, run and tell her that Nam has come home," ordered Mrs. Tran.

Duyen could hardly believe that Nam was home!

"I just brought you food today," her words tumbled out. "No one told me you were coming! What happened?"

"I didn't know either until after you left," Nam explained, his dark eyes sparkling. "As for the supplies, I gave them to my friend in prison. He needed them badly, because he's the skinnest fellow I've ever seen.

"He's been in jail a couple of years already. He's a political prisoner. When he was caught he gave a false identification so he never receives parcels from his family. He's in poor shape. One morning he tried to exercise with the rest of us and fell flat on the ground.

"Duyen, remember the second time you brought me supplies and you were asked to deliver a message? He's the one who sent it. He had just come out of an isolated two-man cell where he'd been for two years."

"When I brought the message to his father, he paid me for that bus trip," Duyen told Nam. "He's a bus driver and was very excited to hear about his son. They had often worried about him."

"Well, he's been complimenting me dozens of times for having such a sweet wife," Nam winked at Duyen. "After you delivered his message he finally got his first package of personal supplies from his family. He received them just a few days ago. I decided to give him my supplies too.

"While I was in jail I saw a number of men leave who took all their food supplies with them. I always thought this was selfish because no doubt they'll have an easier life once they're out of prison. I always felt that being released should have motivated them to share their food with those of us who remained behind.

"So even if your long trip did not benefit me, Duyen it helped someone who has become a very close friend."

Nam and Duyen spent the night in Duyen's home. They talked for hours before falling asleep.

"What are your plans now?" Duyen asked.

"I did a lot of thinking about the future while in prison," Nam replied. "My experience there deepened my determination to leave Vietnam. Duyen, as much as I'd love to stay with you, I still have no other choice but to try again to leave. By fleeing the country I hope to be able eventually to provide for the family and gain freedom for all of us. I feel like that decision is made regardless of my feelings for you."

He spoke slowly and tenderly, aware how much the sensitive and more emotional personality beside him suffered by his absence.

"I know that's probably best," she sighed. "I know that under the present circumstances you don't have the chance to be the kind of husband and father you would like to be."

"That reminds me of a message I need to deliver," Nam said, changing the subject. "I always tried to protect you by telling people that my family was killed and didn't exist any more. I told one man, also a political prisoner, that my family died in grandfather's community. His wife lives there. Tomorrow I have to deliver a message to her."

In the days that followed Nam was too busy to deliver the message, however, so Duyen made it her responsibility.

"I finally was able to contact this lady," Duyen reported later. "She has gone through terrible nightmares and heartaches about her husband's disappearance. She concluded that he was dead and has married another man. Now she's pregnant. She was hysterical when I told her that her first husband is still alive and in prison."

"Similar things happen all the time," Nam stated. "I heard hundreds of sad stories about broken and tangled marriage relationships while I was in prison. It's because of this turmoil and confusion that we have to keep hoping for a brighter tomorrow and keep looking for a way out of it."

The following day Nam visited Tuan, and together with another man, they secretively planned a third escape attempt. Busily they prepared the boat, which belonged to Tuan's father, and made sure one of them was always there to guard it. The preparation site was some thirty-six kilometers out of the city and so Nam was frequently gone from home.

Nam noticed that Duyen became more depressed each day. He tried to comfort her. "Duyen, I really want to spend much time with you and Bao before I leave but it's too risky to be here that much. As far as the government and their records are concerned I don't belong here since I went to the labor camp. I'm on no house occupancy list. It's illegal for anyone to keep me for a night. And if I stay here too regularly I'll get caught again. The neighbors will notice and someone is bound to report me.

"Remember the time I came out of the labor camp? Shortly after that some officers checked my mother's house. I hid on the roof, remember? Then already they highly suspected that unregistered persons might be staying there. I'll have to keep on the move."

Nam stayed with various friends and relatives at random, knowing that in so doing he endangered his hosts. Police could knock on any door at any time of the night to check for unregistered occupants.

Daily Tuan and Nam checked the local news and recorded the ocean tides. Tuan made secret arrangements for others to join them. They hired a carpenter to repair their boat.

When the builder asked for details about their planned

escape by saying he wanted to leave with them, the fellows began to suspect he was a communist spy so they quickly postponed their departure date without informing him. The carpenter did report them and so another group who tried to escape that day was captured as a result.

Little Bao was always excited when Nam came home, for he knew that his father would play and romp with him. Each time Nam left again, Bao cried. Then Duyen would hold him in her arms and cry with him. These were emotional and draining days, for Duyen feared that each farewell would be the last.

Duyen and Nam were careful not to mention the plans to Bao or to Nam's younger brother Jean. The boys were too young to keep a secret of such importance.

Nam also refrained from taking leave of his friends and relatives. "Too many people are getting caught in the midst of their farewells," he told Dyen. "We have to act as if life is just going on as always. I don't want to arouse any suspicion."

Two days before the planned departure Nam dropped in at his mother's home for supper. He announced that he was about to try to escape again.

"I'm willing to risk taking one other family member along," he said. "Could I take Jean?"

"No," Mrs. Tran said. "That's out of the question. If you get caught and he was pressured by the police he would blurt out everything. He's too young, too much of a risk. Besides," she added, "I couldn't part with my youngest child."

Nam's quiet elder sister Phuong spoke up. "I've always dreamed of leaving," she said. "Could I go with you?"

Nam objected immediately. "I don't think you're strong enough. The way your heart has been the last couple of years I don't think you could make it safely."

"Give me a chance," Phuong pleaded. "I'm no good here either. I have nothing to lose."

Nam knew that both Phuong's poor health and tendency to moodiness could make her a difficult companion. Yet he also recognized her determination and powers of endurance once her mind was fixed on a goal.

"Okay, the choice is yours, Phuong," he said reluctantly, "but I'm warning you — you'll have to fend for yourself. It could get tough and I won't be able to pamper you. We're leaving in two days. If you want to go, you'll have to be ready."

The following day Phuong and Nam visited their father in prison. In casual and subdued tones they related their plans to leave the next day. Mr. Tran seemed sad at the news but all three had to hide the pain they felt.

Nam thought of the many hours father and son had once discussed politics and he grieved at the sight of his beloved parent, now cut off from a meaningful role in his life. Even brief encounters like this were artificial, like conversing as strangers. "How I wish I could promise that this would make our future brighter," Nam agonized inwardly.

"I know we may never see each other again . . . but if you make it, it will be worth the separation and the risk," Mr. Tran said, "I don't want you to stay, not the way things are going in Vietnam."

Nam and Phuong rose to go.

"You have my blessing," their father added in a whisper. They smiled and waved farewell with feigned nonchalance. It was the last time Nam saw his father.

Although Nam and Duyen had discussed the subject numerous times before, Nam once more suggested to his wife that she accompany him.

"I know by now how risky it is," he said, "but would you consider coming with me?"

He knew without asking, however, what her answer would be. Even as his responsibility as oldest son motivated him to leave to try to help his family, hers as oldest child of her family also dictated that she stay. The culture in which Nam and Duyen had been raised placed loyalty to parents and family ahead of that to spouse.

"You know I have to stay," she groaned. "Who would visit my father in prison? Who would stay with my little sister?

I can't pass that responsibility on to anyone.

"I know my father has enough money to support himself once he's released from re-education camp. He would gladly give all his money to pay for our family's escape and freedom but I can't leave him. I just can't do that to him."

"I know how you feel about your father," Nam said. "It wouldn't be right for me to insist that you come. If we could trust our relatives to care for your father, it would be different. But they would use all his money for themselves. No, I understand."

"Well," said Duyen courageously, "my brother and sister have already escaped. And perhaps someday I will come too!"

Nam wished he could take his son Bao, but he realized that neither Duyen or his mother would ever allow it.

Nam risked spending his last night May 8, 1979 with Duyen. She was in an extremely distressed state but he was too exhausted to stay awake to comfort her. He slept several hours. Then it was time to leave.

He discovered Duyen had not slept. "What were you thinking about?" he asked.

"I was wondering why my life has to be so sad. My mother died . . ." Duyen broke into tears again. "Father's in prison, my brother and sister have left and now my husband is leaving. Will I ever find happiness again?"

"Oh Duyen," Nam said, putting his arms around her tightly. "You certainly have been through a lot. And I've always admired you for your courage in the face of all these tragedies. They seem to make you stronger and more precious."

Nam held Duyen and Bao closely. He looked at his family with mixed sentiments: love, uncertainty, fear, and hope for a brighter future.

Both Duyen and Bao sobbed. "Even though he's only one-and-a-half, he senses that I'm leaving him," Nam said, smoothing the boy's shiny black hair.

"It's going to be all right," he promised his son. "Be a good boy now. Someday we'll be a happy family again."

"Well Duyen," Nam said, "It's time to say goodbye. I still feel as if this isn't really my decision. It's as if I'm simply following a course laid out for me. I have to follow that course. I would never have chosen to leave you but I've got to go. I'll write you as soon as possible."

10

"TOMORROW WILL BRING US FREEDOM"

The gas, oil, food, and people for the escape trip were waiting at the designated spots along the river. Nam was responsible to pick up seven people along the bank and transport them to the boat.

As Nam approached one rendezvous point he heard a familiar voice.

"Look Anh!" a female voice said excitedly. "I see Nam!"

"And Phuong too! Oh, it will be so good to travel with them," her companion answered.

"We'd better keep calm," the first speaker whispered. "Those fishermen over there may get suspicious if we act too excited."

When the boat reached the bank, Phuong jumped out and scurried to greet the girls, while Nam tied the canoe-like vessel to a tree.

"Well hello, Anh and Thanh," he said. "I didn't know I'd meet you here." He sat down, picked up a pebble and tossed it into the river, thinking, "How did they get here? Do they know I'm escaping? Are they part of my group? I'll have to find out for sure because I'm not planning to get caught again."

Nam began to lightly toss from hand to hand four

grenades wrapped in newspaper. "I have to be careful how I handle these grenades," he whispered to the girls. He watched their faces as he spoke.

Anh sat beside Nam and said quietly, "Our father sent us. But we didn't know you would be here."

"So you want to escape too?"

Both girls nodded. "The communist government confiscated the family shoe factory, as you know," Anh said. "Getting jobs has been next to impossible. Jobs are scarce and with our background, even more difficult. Well, with a family of eleven children, and in-laws and grandchildren, you can imagine what it means to have no income. Our parents realized that the only solution was to have someone leave the country and help from the outside."

"How did you decide who would go?"

"That was the toughest decision. If the men went with their wives and took infants it would increase the risk of getting caught. My parents decided that two adults should go and that they would have to be girls. The whole family chose Mai and me because we were the oldest girls in the family. That decision was made a year ago when Mai was twenty-one and I was twenty-two.

"Secret plans were made, accompanied of course by much apprehension. We left home early one day in May, 1978. We travelled by bus until we reached the river. There we boarded a small boat which was to transport us to a bigger boat further along the river. Unfortunately we were caught by the police before we reached the larger boat.

"That afternoon, to the great surprise of our family, we were home again. Then I resorted to crocheting and embroidery for a government cooperative. That brought in a sliver of food for the family, but most of my wages were kept by the communist party. My parents encouraged us to try again."

Thanh continued, "Every day people try to escape, are discovered and imprisoned, or drowned at sea, but our family was determined that someone risk it once more. This time

Mai would stay home and I, a year younger than she is, would go with Anh. My father argued that the trip with its risks wouldn't be as traumatic for me as for Mai."

She shuddered involuntarily. "I fear that we may be caught and imprisoned. What if we run out of food and starve? Many refugees have been robbed and raped by pirates at sea. What if that happens to us? We may never see our family and friends again." Tears started trickling from Thanh's eyes.

"But what's the point in staying here?" Anh reasoned. "There's always the possibility that we'll make a safe escape and then just think of what we could do to help our family."

Anh took up their story. "A friend of ours came to make arrangements with our father. Father paid the gold and took care of everything. He didn't tell us who was leaving with us, fearing that we might inadvertently say something and be reported before we even leave the country."

Thanh added, "We have a notion that your friend Tuan and maybe our cousin Lan will be on the trip but we have nothing to prove it. Only the immediate family and a few close friends knew of our plans when we left. Upon the wishes of our parents, we went to see a fortune teller two days ago to inquire about our chances of a successful escape. 'You have to trust me,' the fortune teller instructed us, 'or else you will be reported.' We paid our fees and then he gave his predictions.

"He said I would have a lucky life and my chances of escaping were very high. But Anh isn't a lucky person, he said, so I should go with her and I could help her.

"Yesterday we went to the temple to pray to Buddha for protection. We think we will make a safe escape. At least we hope we will." Anh tried to sound convincing.

Nam checked his time and with a quick glance surveyed the surroundings. "We've talked for over an hour already. Four more people are coming but they still have about an hour. Let's get into the canoe and pretend we're fishing so we won't look so conspicuous. We can always catch a few extra fish for our voyage."

The girls picked up their handbags and stepped into the large canoe. All were wearing shabby, worn clothing in order to appear as ordinary country folk. They had a second set of clothing on underneath and carried a few personal items in their bags.

"When did you leave home?" Phuong asked.

"We left at seven this morning." Thanh fought to keep back tears. "Everyone cried when we left. It was just like a funeral. We took the bus to the edge of the city, then walked the last two kilometers. We hid behind that shelter until we noticed you and Nam on the river."

Nam felt it was safe to tell the girls of the plans. "You guessed right," he said. "Tuan has been organizing this escape. His father bought a boat. We'll meet him later on tonight, and I think Lan will be with him too. Tuan has planned carefully and that's why your father couldn't give you more information."

Later when they approached the boat and saw Tuan and Lan the girls smiled in relief. Meeting familiar faces helped remove some of their fears and made them feel more secure.

By 11 p.m. the boat was carrying all nineteen of its passengers and was moving down the river, tugged by the third navigator on a canoe. They would start the boat's motors when they reached a safe distance.

They had an excellent start until they were called by a guard on land to report.

"We aren't going far," Tuan called. But the guard started to shoot at them. Most of the passengers crouched in the storage compartment at the bottom of the boat and Nam scurried into the motor room. He started the motors and accelerated to maximum speed.

The man in the canoe quickly cut the rope joining him to the boat so the canoe would not capsize. After ten minutes they were safe again except that there was no sign of the canoe.

"Where is it? Did he get caught? Should we wait? What if we get caught while waiting?" These were everyone's unspoken questions.

Finally they heard him again. He pulled the canoe in front of the boat. The boat travelled very slowly because they were sure there was another station near them. Very cautiously they lifted their passenger into the boat and his brother-in-law then paddled the canoe in front of them again to scout the passage. At the mouth of the river they parted ways and the couple in the canoe returned to land.

The three navigators huddled for a briefing at the stern of the boat. "We'll have to move at a snail's pace at first and quietly too, so we're not detected by people at the stations," Tuan explained. "This boat is equipped for river travel only, which will make travelling on the ocean extremely risky. I chose to leave in May because that's the time of year when the ocean is most calm."

They meandered further into the mouth of the river. The waves began to roll against them. They were suddenly caught in a fury of wild waves. The navigators tried to keep control and adjust the pace of their little ship to new conditions.

Several hours later one of the two 10 h.p. motors stopped. What could be wrong?

Everyone on the boat was tense. Fear gripped Phuong's heart but she thought, "What does it matter? If I'm lucky I'll gain freedom; if I die I have nothing to lose. Dying is no worse than staying in Vietnam."

Seasickness overcame Nam but he found his way down into the motor room. He closed his eyes and began praying. "God, help us," he pleaded. "Physically I feel like I'm dead. Only my mind works."

"Ouch! That momentum wheel cut my arm. Looks like a deep cut. But I've got to fix this motor before I can attend to my wound." Nam worked quickly to make the adjustments and finally cleared the problem. The engine started again.

With the engine fixed and the waves calmed, the three navigators realized how exhausted they were. They showed Huong how to read the compass so they could get some rest. He was confident about guiding the boat.

Suddenly Nam awoke. Something was amiss. He jerked Huong away from the steering wheel.

"We're going back to land!" he gasped. "Here, let me guide the boat back to the ocean!"

Huong felt embarrassed and slunk away. In the meantime Tuan came to investigate the commotion.

"Everyone is sound asleep," Nam observed after they had matters under control again.

"Yes," Tuan said. "It's deathly quiet, isn't it."

They were silent for a few minutes.

"Thinking about anything in particular?" Nam asked.

"No, nothing too important." Tuan hesitated, then blurted out, "I'm wondering how Lan will make out."

"Ah! So that's it. We're escaping the country and you're thinking of a girl." Nam grinned. "I was wondering how you managed to persuade Lan to come with only a day's notice."

"She's been very disappointed with the way the communists treat her family," Tuan said seriously. "She's twenty-two and still can't get a job. She's been staying with her grandmother's sister in Saigon for a year already because she's tired of being dependent on her parents."

"Do her parents know that she's with us?"

"That's what bothers me, Nam. Lan didn't have time to go and bid her family good-bye."

"But I understand that her parents had been encouraging her to leave a long time ago."

"That's right, they've often discussed it. Since none of her sisters wanted to leave they told her to find a means of escaping," Tuan stated. "She did get her grandmother's sister's blessing and I hope Lan won't regret that she accepted this offer."

"Hey Tuan! Did you see that?" Nam exclaimed.

"What?" Tuan peered into the darkness, bewildered.

"We just barely scraped by one of the government nets!"

"I didn't know there were any nets this far out."

"I had heard about them but had totally forgotten about them." Nam shook his head, filled with awe. "This certainly must be God's hand guiding us. If I had known it was there I'm not sure I would have been able to steer past in this darkness."

Once they were on the sea, away from Vietnam, Nam felt a sense of relief and joy. Although they were not yet safe, for Nam, the climactic point of the journey had been reached. He was away from the stifling clutches of communism.

In the days to come he occasionally swam beside the boat and once he touched some playful dolphins.

But there were also problems and tensions. Two days later one of the motors began to run very roughly and ruined the sea compass hanging on the shaft.

Upon investigation they discovered a bolt had broken on the shaft and caused the propeller to pull out of position. Fortunately it had not been a large tear. But it needed to be fixed from the outside of the ship. Nam checked carefully for sharks and dived into the water. Tuan, however, had brought a land compass which they then used. It did not work accurately so it left them rather uncertain about their whereabouts.

"Well, if it isn't one thing it's another," Nam remarked later when he went to the bottom of the boat. "There's a leak in the boat."

Busily he bailed out water for an hour. He saw the pasengers sitting idly.

"Listen you people just sitting there! Why don't you do something?" Nam demanded, irritated.

"We paid for the trip," Phuong snapped back.

"You guys planned this voyage and you should know how to handle things," someone else retorted.

"That's right, we planned it," Nam responded angrily, "but we also planned on your cooperation. We five crew men are working all the time and the rest of you just sit and complain. At this rate we'll never make a safe landing anywhere. We need your cooperation if we don't want to drown."

"Now Nam," Phuong scolded, "you needn't be so hard on us. Some of us aren't feeling so great, you know. How do you expect us to help you?"

"Boy, do I feel like throwing my sister into the sea!" Nam

muttered. To Phuong he said, "I warned you that this would be risky business and I want you to start cooperating right now."

"Okay," Phuong sighed. "What do you want us to do?"

"All of you take turns dipping out the water. We'll try to keep the boat moving," Nam suggested.

"That lecture helped," noted Nam to Tuan later. "It's good to see everyone helping along for a change."

That night the motor which had acted up previously died completely. The crew members decided that they could do nothing about it. Propelling the boat with one motor considerably slowed their progress.

"Oh well, we can be thankful that one motor is in excellent condition," they agreed.

The days dragged by. Each sunset meant the end of another long weary hot day. Nearly everyone got sick to his stomach and vomited. The odor only made their stomachs churn more. Clothes, hair and faces became caked with vomit, perspiration, dirt and smoke from the motors.

"How are you feeling Thanh? Your eyes are getting redder and bigger all the time," Anh asked with sisterly concern.

"I feel terrible. I'm getting skinnier every day and my eyebrows are growing like monkeys!" Thanh laughed.

A hole in the back of the boat served as a toilet. There were no facilities to bathe or even wash properly: a terrible burden for many of the passengers, accustomed to fastidious cleanliness.

"I'm sure glad I managed to take three sets of clothing so I don't need to wear the same thing all the time," Lan said, trying to be positive. "I only wish I had brought more medication for seasickness. Some of you could use some more."

When the girls could not stand the stench and the heat in the enclosed passenger section any longer they would lie on the deck closely crammed together in crouched positions. With their hands they held empty rice bags over their bodies to prevent sunburn.

The fifth day at sea Tuan pointed to something in the

distance. "I think I see a fishing boat. We're in desperate need of food and water. Perhaps we can get some supplies."

As they approached the ship Nam exclaimed, "That boat must be ten times the size of ours! I see Indian-like men on deck but I can't identify from what country the boat comes."

With one of the engines dead it was difficult to catch up with the ship. Everyone stood on deck and waved desperately for help.

"I hope they'll have mercy on us," Anh moaned. "We could all use a little food and water to give us energy to go on."

Nam instructed one of the men to prepare the gun and two grenades in case they would be needed for defense.

As they neared the fishing vessel it stopped moving. The strangers motioned them to stay away but the weary refugees continued to call out, "Help us! We need water! We need food!"

When Nam and Tuan recognized the flag of Thailand they turned quickly to the women. "Get to the bottom of the boat," they commanded. "You may be robbed or raped."

The girls, however, did not obey orders. They were too sick and hot to care about anything. "I'd rather die than hide in that hot stinky room below," Phuong stated.

"They can throw me into the sea, but I'm not going into the bottom of this boat," Thanh added.

"We better leave them alone. They might kill us," Tuan said imploringly, fearful of what could happen.

"We have nothing to lose. If we don't get help now we'll die. If we talk to them we might die too, but there's always the chance that we get help," Nam persisted. "I'll go on the ship. I'll take the responsibility on myself for whatever happens. Does anyone here speak English? We may have to communicate with these people in English."

Nam guided their small boat along the rear right of the huge fishing boat. Nobody dared leave with Nam. "I hoped that at least one man would come with me," he thought. "But they're all too frightened."

He ventured out of the boat. "I must be a horrible sight —

my body and clothes penetrated with oil and dirt after a week at sea," he thought as he climbed up the cable extending from a fishing net to the ship. He made sure there was no way for the fishermen to raid the refugee boat.

"Getting onto this large fishing boat is like moving from a small town to a civilized city," Nam noticed. "Everything is perfectly clean. We have a piece of junk in comparison. I don't see how we've made it this far."

Nam's fellow passengers waved at Nam. He faced their direction but stared past them, trying to get himself under control to make sure he would make the proper move.

He jumped when someone tapped him on the shoulder. Quickly Nam turned around. He saw a dark brown-skinned fisherman with a friendly expression.

Nam wasted no time. He spoke in English. The man responded in Vietnamese. For a second Nam froze. "Surely this isn't a Vietnamese boat. If it is we'll all be killed right on the spot," he thought.

The man detected Nam's fear and identified himself as a Vietnamese born in Thailand.

Nam was relieved. Hurriedly he explained the situation. "We are heading towards freedom. We will be grateful to you all our lives if you will open your hearts and help us get to the mainland. We escaped a country where we had no freedom. You have all the freedom you want, so please help us. Could you possibly tow us to the Malaysian coast? We'll manage from there."

"I can't answer that question," responded the fisherman, "but I'll direct you to the captain's office."

"I can't do anything for you," the captain said after Nam repeated his request. "If the Thailand police would find out about our helping you, I would be imprisoned immediately."

Nam continued pleading for mercy until Ninh, who was more fluent in English, came to join him.

"What we could do for you people right now is to show you how to get there and ensure that your compass coordination is right," the captain finally suggested. "We will also give you some fresh water and fish. You guys look like you haven't eaten in years!"

The captain showed Nam their location on the map and what course to take. "You're presently some hundred kilometers from the mainland," he explained.

"Thank you for the water, the ice, fresh fish, cigarettes, and instructions," Ninh said on behalf of the group.

Nam was so excited about the assistance they had received that it spurred him to make another attempt to fix the dead motor. Eventually he succeeded.

New excitement was in the air. The girls boiled the fish in salt water and everyone feasted. "This gives me new energy and courage," Phuong said cheerfully. "Be careful not to eat too much because we'll be seasick again," Anh warned.

"At ten kilometers per hour we should get to land before dark," the navigators calculated. Progress was slower than they anticipated, however. Darkness fell, but they decided not to use their one and only light, for fear of being spied by pirates. Although reading the compass was difficult in the blackness it was a night to remember. "All I can see are the stars, sky, and bubbles of water stirred up by the boat. How peaceful these surroundings are. God has brought us safely this far and tomorrow will bring us freedom forever."

This joy was soon drenched with fear.

"A storm is coming!" Nam warned the passengers. "Get down into the boat!"

"Oh Nam, it's impossible to stay down there," they protested again. "It's much too hot and smelly."

Suddenly it began to rain. The rain turned into a wild storm. Fear gripped each one in the bottom of the boat where they had taken refuge after all.

"God, protect us from the storm," many prayed.

The excitement Nam had felt earlier in the day was still very real to him. Fighting with the angry waves was a challenge, one that he and two other men who stayed up with him thoroughly enjoyed.

"The boat has both motors running. I think we can beat

those waves!" he thought confidently. "But it's sure hard to see. The pelting rain and the wind are obstructing my vision; I have to hold my hand over my eyes so I can watch the waves. And if we get hit sideways by one of those we'll sink just like that."

"Do you want me to read the compass?" Tuan shouted over the crashing sounds of the storm.

"If you can! Tell me how far we're off course!"

One man ran down to the engine room to pump out the water. Since the water level was quite high he was able to use the motor's pump to remove the water. "Everything is in good shape," he reported back later.

"I've got the greatest team ever," Nam thought proudly.

The women were too fearful to sleep. Their hopes of reaching the mainland had been high and yet now they doubted if they would survive the storm.

Soon the tempest calmed. Everyone was exhausted. The day had been unusually eventful and mixed feelings made them all weary.

One by one they fell asleep. Those who stayed awake peered into the distance until they saw mountains on the horizon. After some time they saw lights. Excitement mounted again and the mood of happy expectation awakened the sleepers. Shortly before dawn they reached the shores of Malaysia.

11

"WHERE SHALL WE GO?"

"Are you drunk Nam?" Tuan teased when they stepped on to land. Used to the rocking motion of the ship Nam struggled to keep his balance on the firm earth.

"You're not so steady yourself!" he responded, laughing.

Gradually they gained their "land legs." Nam, Tuan and a third man set off into the city to find a police station.

A bus whizzed past Nam's ear. "Whew!" he gasped. "That was a close shave. Looks like traffic in Malaysia drives on the left side."

Their first stop was a store. The salespeople immediately recognized them as refugees and asked if they had any gold. Although they knew no Vietnamese and very little English, they then tried their best to explain how to find the police office.

The men continued their expedition, all three walking in the middle of the road. An oncoming motorbike driver spotted them and made a sudden U-turn to follow them. He stared, aghast.

At daybreak they met a mother and her teenage daughter. "Do you know where we can find a police station?" Nam inquired.

The woman screamed, grabbed her daughter and hurried away.

"Our filthy appearance is attracting attention and even scaring people," the wanderers concluded.

They reached the main street of the city. They approached a college student but he too seemed frightened. He shook his head and crossed the street.

A block later they finally met a man who would stop and direct them to the police station. As the refugees entered the building the police officers glanced at each other in horror.

Nam introduced themselves. "We left Vietnam in search of freedom," he said. "Can you help us? Is there a refugee camp nearby?"

The men were instructed to first wash themselves. They scrubbed and scrubbed but even warm water and soap failed to completely remove the smudge and grime which had saturated their skin.

Then two friendly policemen drove Nam and his friends back to the waterfront. The other members of the group still waited on the boat.

While the three scouts were gone a policeman had come to record everyone's name. He left with the message, "We don't want any foreigners to land in our country. We don't want to get into trouble. We want to keep peace in our country, so don't disturb us. Stay on the boat until you get further instructions."

When Nam and his comrades approached their boat a Malaysian military squad began to threaten and beat the young men. "Get back into that boat. And if you have any guns, we'll kill you," ordered the commander.

"Throw out the ammunition," Nam mouthed as he neared the boat. Fortunately someone understood and managed to throw the weapons overboard, so, while they were still visible from the boat, the squad members did not notice.

Tuan continued pleading, "Please have mercy on us. We've been under the hot sun a whole week. We desperately need shelter and nourishment. If you won't help all of us please have pity on the baby and the pregnant woman we have with us. Doesn't the baby's continuous screaming arouse any sympathy in you?"

"All right. We'll get you some bread and milk, but don't you dare get out of your boat until we've made arrangements for your further transportation," ordered the task force commander.

"Why couldn't we wait under those trees?" grumbled Thanh.

"I don't understand why they're so picky," Nam echoed. "If only we could get out of the sun. Those trees look like they're reaching out to us in pity."

Late that afternoon several cars transferred the weary refugees to a temporary camp by the seashore. They received the basic provisions to live there for two weeks. They slept in tents.

On May 29 the group was transferred to a refugee camp on the island of Pulau Bidong, a small hill protruding out of the sea. While travelling there they encountered another bad storm and Nam lost most of his already limited belongings.

Pulau Bidong, an island of about two-and-a-half square kilometers was mainly forest. The camp shelters covered about one third of the island, which could temporarily house over 40,000 refugees.

The refugees' first duty on arriving was to register. The registrar quickly acquired the needed information and then explained, "The number CG2305 represents your whole group. It signifies your date of arrival. The number 423 is your boat number because you are the four-hundred-and-twenty-third boat load of refugees from Vietnam, Cambodia and Laos to come to this island. Whenever we have a message for you we will call you over the public address system using these numbers."

Nam inquired about Duyen's sister who had escaped Vietnam earlier. The officer located her and directed her to Nam using their serial and boat numbers. They greeted one another happily and eagerly exchanged news and experiences.

"I'm doing very well," she exclaimed. "I've applied to go to the United States and I'm hoping to leave in a few days. I hope Duyen can join you soon. Maybe we will meet again in America."

During their stay in Pulau Bidong, Nam had many opportunities to exchange stories with other refugees. Hearing some of the terrible experiences of others made him realize how well their escape had gone. In retrospect it seemed miraculous. He heard of women who had been raped many times, of robberies, deprivation and death.

Now that they were safe at the refugee camp the new arrivals proceeded to apply for sponsorship to another country.

"The first job is getting your identification cards processed," the registrar informed them. "We will register you by families. That way you'll be able to stay together wherever you go."

"You'll have to make a quick decision," stated the registrar. "Either you register as a married man or as a family with your sister Phuong. If you register as a single man you'll have a better chance of being sponsored plus you can stay with your sister. You can always change your documents after you arrive in whatever country you will go to."

Nam struggled, realizing he had only a few moments to decide. He had to choose between his wife and his sister.

He turned to Phuong. "What do you say?" he asked.

"I don't want to be left on my own," she said, giving him a pleading look.

The registrar prompted, "Don't worry. It's just a temporary identification. This is being done all the time. You can change it as soon as you reach your destination."

"It seems the most logical thing to do," Nam reasoned. "I can't leave Phuong alone now that I took her this far. I'll do anything to get out of here sooner and help my family. I just hope it won't make life more difficult for Duyen than it already is."

"Okay, make a joint identification for Phuong and myself," Nam consented.

Of Nam's group of nineteen people about half found friends and relatives in the refugee camp with whom they could find shelter. The first nights had been spent on the beach. In the mornings they awoke with worms crawling over their bodies and people thronging around them.

Nam and Tuan were well-used to fending for themselves, and it did not take them long to borrow a saw and axe and purchase some nails. They headed up the mountain into the jungle to cut trees for a shelter. Climbing barefooted uphill and through thick bush was more difficult than Nam had anticipated. Although their trail was partially cleared by previous refugees it was still almost impassable. The young men had finished the liter of drinking water each had taken along soon after they set out. They did not reach their destination that day.

The second day the fellows were better prepared for the obstacles. They knew they would have to go to the top of the mountain if they were to find trees straight and large enough for their purpose; the lower slopes were already picked over. They cut and trimmed the logs, and peeled off the rough bark in order to ease pulling and pushing the logs through the jungle and down the mountain.

"I've never done anything like this before," commented Tuan, wiping the sweat from his forehead.

"It's hard work but we're not doing too badly for amateurs," Nam replied.

They assembled enough logs for a shelter about four meters long and two meters wide. Then they drove in the stakes. Because of the steep slope the floor and back wall met at ground level. In front, the floor was six feet above the ground. The walls, floors and ceiling were made by nailing the round logs together, side by side. They collected enough money to buy plastic to cover the roof and two of the walls.

The shack was divided into two sleeping quarters, one for the women and the other for the men. They stored their few belongings under the front part of their shelter.

The young carpenters split logs lengthwise to make a smoother floor. It also served as their beds. "My bed is rather bumpy, I must say," chuckled Nam after the first night, "with no blankets or extra clothes to use for cushioning."

Swarms of mosquitoes invaded their shack during the night. Those refugees who had sufficient provisions covered their faces with extra clothing, stuffed their hands into their pockets and wrapped plastic bags around their legs to ward off the small vicious marauders.

During the day the mosquitoes disappeared but were then replaced by flies. They were everywhere. "I'm surprised there's no malaria on this island," Nam remarked.

"Maybe it has something to do with it being a recently inhabited island," Tuan suggested. "I heard the other day that it isn't even a year ago since the first people moved onto this island."

"I suppose you're right, Tuan."

"Nam, I've been thinking we'll have to do something with our shack. It's beginning to shift more every day."

"You know what happened to me this afternoon?" Nam laughed. "While I was taking my nap someone else's log came sailing right into our shack. Man did I wake up fast and get out of there!"

"I guess building our shack on the open trail wasn't such a great idea after all." Tuan grinned.

"It sure saved time though," chuckled Nam. "We didn't have to clear the ground like we would have had to, had we built elsewhere. And I must say I rather like our location." Their improvised shelter was the highest of all the camp houses in that particular area. They were also situated beside a waterfall, which gurgled and sang. "It's pleasant, even beautiful," he continued.

"Nam, you know I've been thinking that we should make our own well. The water from the falls is too dirty because of all the people who do their laundry and take their baths at the top of the stream. And I hate going to the dock where water is supplied."

"I agree! Last time we went to get water we had spilled half of our tank of water by the time we dragged it up here over all the stumps and around all the other shacks. Not to mention my smashed toes!"

"Going up the mountain for water is no better," Tuan added. "Half an hour to get to the top. Another half hour to fill our container. I don't particularly enjoy that as a daily chore."

The next morning Tuan and Nam secured their shack by anchoring the corners to nearby tree stumps with rope.

Then they set about to dig their well. "We might as well experiment," thought Nam. They dug between the waterfall and the house, about a meter from the house. At about half a meter they hit a rock which they diligently excavated and then dug deeper.

"I don't believe this," Nam shouted suddenly. "There's water down there!

Tuan lowered a bucket and pulled up fresh clean water. "We sure were lucky to hit a water vein this high," the fellows exclaimed.

Once their facilities for basic survival were established Nam turned his attention to his application for sponsorship.

Each country had a list of prerequisites for accepting refugees. The refugees were interviewed in the order of their arrival at the camp.

Phuong and Nam discussed where they should go. "I think it would be wisest to go to the USA because father worked with the American army during the Vietnamese war," Nam argued. "That should make it easier for our parents to be accepted later too. I've heard that their first choice is refugees who already have blood relatives in the USA, or are orphans. Their second choice is those who worked for the American army or their children under twenty-one. Thirdly, they take people who worked for the Vietnamese government. Refugees with distant relatives in the States fall into the fourth category. The last category is those who don't fit any of the first four situations but just want to leave the country. I really don't think we should have any problem being accepted by the American delegation."

"Another reason why America is a good choice, Phuong added "is because they seem to put the most effort into sponsoring refugees. Their representatives work from sunrise to sunset and come more frequently than any other country's delegations."

"We should be called for an interview with the Americans very soon. They're starting with boat 400 so there are only twenty-three more until our turn."

As it happened, the American delegation temporarily ceased interviewing shortly after boat number four hundred due to a change in the immigration policies of the United States.

One evening when discussing the group's future, Tuan said, "I hear that anyone falling into the fifth category of American prerequisites has to go to the United Nations refugee camp in the Philippines for three years before they can go to the U.S.A."

"I think that's just a threat," Nam stated. "Besides, some people say they've waited here so long that three years won't make that much difference."

"Have you ever considered another country, Nam?" Tuan asked.

"We'll have to start considering that," Nam replied. "If the American delegation doesn't start interviewing soon Phuong will be twenty-one and we won't qualify for their second category anymore."

"What about Australia?" Phuong suggested. "A close cousin of mine went there a few years ago to study and I'd like to meet her. Though my next choice would be France where mother has relatives."

"I wouldn't mind going to France myself," said Anh. "In fact, I have an uncle there who I'm sure would gladly accept us."

The next time the Australian delegation visited the camp Nam's group applied. But they were never called for an interview.

Their third application was made to France. The French delegation promised to interview anyone who spoke French. A problem arose, however, when the delegates asked for precise addresses of relatives in France and no one had addresses along.

"I guess that's it as far as France is concerned," Anh

concluded.

A sense of panic overcame Nam. Where should he go?

"Why not try Canada?" a friend suggested. "That's where I'm going!"

"I have no relatives in Canada," answered Nam, "I know no one there."

"I don't have close relatives anywhere abroad, so it doesn't matter to me where we go," Lan commented, "but I want to stay with this little group. Canada sounds okay to me. I think it will be easy to be accepted there and the two Canadian languages, English and French, seem like easy languages to learn."

Thanh and Anh decided that they too wanted to stay with Nam and Phuong, and asked him to handle their applications. "Canada is all right for us," they said. "We have friends and relatives spread throughout the world by now so it doesn't really matter where we go as long as we are free and can help our families back home."

When Nam decided to apply for Canadian sponsorship he learned that Canada's first choice was refugees who already had relatives in that country. "You are welcome to apply, but we are only up to boat number 200 with interviews," a Canadian immigration officer told Nam. "And some boats have as many as 400 people so those interviews take several days. It will be a long time before we get to boat 423."

Nam returned to the shelter and informed the rest of his group about the long wait ahead of them. "The Canadian interviews aren't nearly as detailed as the American ones," he reported. "I suppose that's because they weren't so involved in the Vietnam war."

"What bothers me," he continued, "is that the big boats always seem to take priority and many of those passengers happen to have relatives in Canada." He tried to cheer himself and the others by saying, "I also heard that Canada has said she'll take 50,000 refugees. We may be lucky enough to be one of them."

"I wonder what it would be like to live in Canada, among all those big people?" Tuan asked. "Have you noticed that the

Canadian delegates are bigger than other delegates?"

"I noticed that today," Nam replied. "I'm sure some of their delegates weigh over ninety kilograms."

"I guess that means there's no shortage of food in Canada," Thanh said.

"Yeh! Let's go to Canada!" everyone cheered.

Nam had written numerous short letters to Duyen. Now that their basic needs were taken care of and they had little to do besides wait to be accepted by any country he decided it was time for a more detailed letter.

July 19, 1979

Dear Duyen,

It is over two months now since we last saw each other. A lot has happened since then.

Sometimes I swim around the island in the afternoons and take naps. I spend a good portion of my nights studying French and English.

I was able to borrow some books from friends. They use them during the day, but they let me use their books during the night. I study mostly by lamplight. I make a list of all my problem words, run down the hill in the morning to borrow another friend's dictionary, look up my problem words, make notes, and then quickly return the dictionary so others can use it.

Someone offered me a job teaching French. He said this would give me access to the library books that are reserved for staff only. I feel nervous about standing in front of twenty to thirty people but I think I'll take the job.

The Catholic church conducts daily Mass which I attend once a week. I used to borrow a friend's pants to go. I had only two shirts and two pairs of shorts. Yesterday I received some pants from a shipment of clothing sent by the U.S.A. So now I can use my own pants for Mass.

In general people here get extremely bored while waiting for sponsorship. There's not much to do while waiting. The girls often go for walks when it isn't too hot. They also do a lot of swimming. Often it is too hot to sleep at night so they just talk till late and then sleep till about ten next morning. During the hottest part of the day they sit under the trees and fan themselves. On windy and rainy days they sit in their shelters. They do their laundry in a nearby stream and do their own cooking.

Getting around on this island is quite a job. It took me three weeks to learn how to get from one end of the island to the other. All the shelters look so much alike that it's difficult to establish any landmarks.

When I met your sister she showed me where she lived. Later I forgot how to get to her place. I met her in a crowd about a week later and then she directed me to her place again. She is doing very well. Since we arrived she's been hoping to leave for America any day.

Last night I couldn't sleep because of the mosquitoes. I decided to go sleep by the ocean. Normally it takes me ten minutes to get from here to the shore but last night I stumbled around in the darkness for an hour before I finally reached the shore line.

By now we're so used to walking on slopes all the time that it would feel rather strange to walk on level ground. I suppose we must all be lopsided because we never walk on any flat surface around here!

Every two or three days the Red Cross supplies the camp with food. Each boat number is announced in turn and then two members pick up our rations of rice, vegetables and meat prepackaged in cans and bags. The food is supplied through the United Nations and the Malaysian government.

Sometimes the food doesn't arrive on time because of storms at sea. That means 'no food' unless we have money to buy more luxurious varieties at the Malaysian market stands. Many people, including Lan, have traded their jewelry for food.

The girls are in constant fear of contagious diseases, which are increasing and I too fear that if we have to wait here much longer we will contact some disease which would disqualify us for any sponsorship. It is impossible for the few doctors and nurses to treat all the sick, even though they work around the clock. There is a shortage of medicine. The seriously ill are transferred to a French ship serving as a hospital.

Sadness, depression, and tears are very much a part of everyday life. Thanh is more depressed than Lan, Anh and Phuong. Sometimes Thanh cries day and night wishing to die rather than continue this kind of existence. The other girls are becoming concerned about her mental state.

Daily broadcasts announce the arrival of foreign delegations. The different delegations come every two to four weeks and stay two or three days.

We are eagerly waiting every day to be accepted for sponsorship. I'll write you again when I can send you a permanent address.

Take care of yourself and Bao. I miss you every day.

Love,

Nam

During their third month on the island various acquaintances of Nam's group started to leave for other countries. It made those that waited even more restless.

The shack began to sag. When it seemed beyond repair the girls abandoned it and moved into a better shelter donated by friends who left the island.

Tuan and Nam, however, chose to stay in their shabby shelter.

Nam decided to apply to every country that had a delegation at camp, except for countries with Slavic languages. He felt these languages were too difficult to learn.

Germany, he learned was too crowded. He applied to Holland and was interviewed, but received no notice of acceptance.

Sponsorship seemed to elude them. "We made it this far, but how will we ever get out of here?" Nam wondered. "Many of our friends are leaving but nothing seems to work out for us. No acceptance from France or Holland. The Australian delegations are too slow. And we're getting too old to qualify for the United States."

Canada seemed the only positive option left. Nam volunteered to work for their delegation whenever they were on the island. He filed cards, listing names under different priority groupings, or did translation work.

After helping the Canadian delegation for about a month whenever they were on the island, one of the delegates asked, "Nam, would you like to go to Canada?"

"Yes, I want to," was Nam's quick response, "but our boat number has never been called."

"I'll see if I can't get your application processed very shortly," the delegate assured him.

The day finally arrived when Nam, Phuong, Anh, Thanh, Lan, and Tuan as well as six other members of their boat group were accepted for Canada. Two of the couples were automatically accepted because they had relatives in Canada. The rest of their boat group of nineteen were accepted by the United States.

Tuan had one wish to fulfill before leaving the island. He had learned to love Lan and wanted to marry her.

One evening as Tuan and Lan walked along the beach he broached the subject. "I have come to admire you a lot, Lan" he said. "Once we get to Canada I would like to settle down with you as my wife. Would you marry me, Lan?" Tuan had been a good friend and had helped her a lot, Lan realized. But she did not feel ready for marriage.

"There's too much on my mind right now. And I have my family in Vietnam who desperately need my help. I have to think about them," she said, "I just can't say yes now."

Tuan's voice was serious, "Even though we're both going to Canada, our ways may part there because we're sponsored by different groups. But my devotion for you will continue growing in spite of your present feelings and our possible separation. I'm not going to give you up now. I will keep on waiting, just like we've waited so long for acceptance to Canada."

12

"WELCOME TO CANADA"

Before Nam and his group left the Pulau Bidong Refugee Camp with many others, the communications director delivered a farewell speech.

"Dear friends," he said, "we're gathered to say good-bye to another group leaving for a new country. We will all miss you, because we have spent several important months together on this island. We have shared good and bad experiences.

"We all know why we were here. We were willing to trade our lives for one thing: freedom.

"It is not likely that we will meet again, but we're all striving for the same goal wherever we are: to prepare to return to the country where we once belonged. We have to be ready to return and revitalize our country which has been ruined after so many years of violation and hatred.

"We wish you the best of luck and on behalf of all the others on this island we wish you a safe trip to your third country."

It was a difficult farewell because those still in the camp had to continue waiting. They longed for the same news of sponsorship. Some had waited much longer than Nam's group but were not allowed to leave because of health problems.

The girls, Phuong, Anh, Thanh, and Lan, shed tears when they boarded the boat that would transport them from Pulau Bidong. Now that it was time to leave they realized how attached they were to the camp, how they had enjoyed life there, how many memories they were leaving.

Nam could not understand why they cried. To him the last months seemed like a dream. He thanked God for his protection in the past and wondered what it would be like to settle in the unknown northern country of Canada where they had no relatives nor acquaintances. Would Canada give him the freedom he searched for? Would it provide a future for his family? Suddenly Nam too felt nostalgic. He missed Pulau Bidong. It at least was familiar. Slowly the island faded out of his vision.

This time the sea voyage was no matter of life or death. Travel on a thousand-passenger ship was much different than on a twenty-passenger boat. The huge ship rocked differently than the small ship did five months ago and Nam and the girls got thoroughly seasick. By the time they reached the mainland of Malaysia they were too fatigued to even feel hungry.

They boarded a bus at Kuala Trengganu at sundown and headed for Kuala Lumpur, the capital of Malaysia. All the passengers were destined for Canada. The speedy bus ride on the left side thoroughly frightened the Vietnamese. They thought no one would survive the collisions which seemed sure to happen. To their relief they arrived safely in Kuala Lumpur the next morning.

Malaysia was a lovely hilly country and Kuala Lumpur was a beautiful city. The climate differed from Vietnam in that the nights were cooler.

Their next stay was a tin-roofed barrack next to a convent, where they went through health examinations for ten days. The Malaysian authorities allowed each person two square meters for sleeping and storage space and each family had a limit of six liters of water per day. Any unauthorized person leaving the camp would be brutally beaten or get his head shaved.

Nam was allowed to go to the city center to have some teeth pulled. While in the city he and his friend made comparisons to Vietnam. "These people wear better clothes," Nam said. "They must be richer than the average Vietnamese person."

Nam and his Chinese-Vietnamese friend had some time to shop before they had to return on the five o'clock bus. They spoke Vietnamese to each other, and to strangers who did not understand, Nam spoke English or his friend spoke Chinese.

"I love this place," commented Nam's friend. "It feels so free, so different from Vietnam. And there's so much we could buy fairly cheaply." Nam bought several post cards and mailed one to Duyen.

After ten days the refugees were moved to a transitional camp where they would wait for their call to the airport. Here they met one of the two couples from their group that had left Pulau Bidong earlier. The other couple had already left for Canada. They spent four pleasant days in the camp.

The long-awaited date of departure for Canada finally came. After Nam presented his papers to the officers at the airport he was assigned as an interpreter again. He sat in the front of the DC 9 jet, which held some 200 refugees.

A mood of excitement filled the aircraft, subdued only slightly when the captain announced they were flying near Vietnam. "Take a good look at your country, Vietnam," he said. "Perhaps it is the last time you will ever see it."

"This is it for Vietnamese," Nam thought. "From now on I'll speak only English and French." Nam wished now that he had worked harder at his English and French. Yet he was glad to know he could use what his father had invested in him: time and education. "My father always wanted me to get post-secondary education in France or Australia. I'll fulfill his wishes for me in Canada. How I wish he could be with me right now."

The refugees left Malaysia on a Sunday morning. When they reached Edmonton it was still Sunday morning. "Coming to Canada made us one day younger!" Nam joked with other passengers.

They were given instructions for landing and exiting.

"Please put on any extra jackets you have. The temperature here in Edmonton is close to freezing. You will soon discover that the only free things in Canada are ice and snow."

"I don't need to worry about putting on extra clothes, because I don't have any extra clothes," Nam thought.

Everyone ran into the terminal building shivering, except for Nam in his short sleeves. "It's not as cold as I thought it would be," he said to the Canadian immigration officer, laughing.

The refugees gladly shook hands with the Canadian officers who greeted them with: "Welcome to Canada. We hope you will feel at home and enjoy living here."

From the airport they were transferred to a nearby army base. Most of the refugees arrived with a small handbag containing two sets of clothes, sandals, and their documents. At the army base the Red Cross agency distributed boots, jackets, towels, gloves, and other winter clothing as well as soap, toothbrushes, and toothpaste. Everyone had to clear another medical examination.

Suddenly the refugees were in a new culture, climate, and land. The first days were filled with new and strange experiences.

"These streetcars, subways, and vending machines are things we have never seen before," Anh told one of the Red Cross workers through the help of an interpreter. "We find them most interesting."

"Getting change for a dollar bill from a machine is something we had read about but never saw," Thanh added.

Nam saw his first real cowboy. "I've seen cowboys in western movies but I thought they were a thing of the past!" he said. "But I see that modern cowboys drive Cadillacs instead of horses!"

Nam, always a keen lover of nature, found the adornment of the trees in their fall colors even more beautiful than he had imagined. "I've seen pictures of autumn trees but I never realized how glorious they are in reality."

The refugees also had disappointments. "How will we ever

get used to this cold weather?" Lan worried. "It's only October and the weather is supposed to get much colder."

"And to not know the language!" Anh complained. "We can't talk to anyone without Nam having to interpret for us."

"How will I ever be able to communicate with Canadians? How will I ever get a job?" Thanh cried. "I want to go back to Vietnam where I know the language. I want to be with my family."

For the first few nights the newcomers suffered from jet lag. They slept during the day.

"This night I'm going to watch television because I won't be able to sleep again," Nam told the girls one evening. When he entered the lounge he discovered a roomful of wide-awake people with the same problem.

"I found out that we're going to Stratton, Ontario," Nam informed the girls. They diligently studied a map of Canada. They could not find Stratton.

The girls looked at Nam, their eyes full of questions.

"That's all I know," he said. "We'll be sponsored by a Friesen family in Stratton, Ontario."

13

"NOW YOU HAVE FIVE MORE CHILDREN"

Nam and the four girls — Anh, Thanh, Lan and Phuong — boarded a jet in Edmonton early on October 31, 1979. They had a one-hour stopover in Manitoba's capital.

New sights and strange customs still bombarded their senses. Nam saw a man remove his shoes and prop his feet on an airport table. Nam quickly turned aside. "How uncivilized!" he thought. "I'd never see that in Vietnam. We've always been taught to sit up straight with our feet down in public."

From Winnipeg the five young people flew to Thunder Bay, Ontario and then backtracked westward on a five-hour bus trip to Fort Frances.

They were greatly puzzled to see children walking the streets in weird and colorful costumes.

"Well, they seem friendly, so maybe it's the way Canadians here dress," Nam concluded the discussion. Later they learned they had witnessed the eccentricities of Halloween!

They also saw their first snowfall. "This is fantastic!" Nam told the bus driver enthusiastically. "A truly amazing sight!"

By the time they reached Fort Frances after 10 p.m. the travellers were exhausted, as they had been so many times since they left their homeland.

"I'm almost too tired to care about who will sponsor us or to imagine what life will be like once we reach our destination," Anh sighed when she stepped off the bus.

They were confident that life would have new meaning and many opportunities but what showed on their faces now was weariness, fear and the emotional stresses of the past half-year.

The immigration officers, their sponsors Jake and Mary Friesen, and their son Phil and Justina Friesen welcomed Nam and his group. Some members of the Nussbaumer family, fluent in the French language, had also come to greet them.

Once the immigration paper work was done they piled into three vehicles and proceeded to Stratton, their final destination, another fifty kilometers away.

Nam travelled with Phil and Justina and did not hesitate to get involved in a conversation in spite of the great effort it took him to follow the fast English Phil and Justina spoke. The girls knew French better than English so they drove along with the Nussbaumer family to Emo and then went along with the elder Friesens for the last stretch, arriving in their home at 11:30 p.m.

The girls could not understand enough English to communicate effectively at first. Nam, on the other hand, had little problem carrying on a conversation in English, so he quickly became the interpreter between the Friesens and the group of girls.

Jake Friesen introduced himself and his wife and said, "We have twelve children."

"Now you have five more children," Nam joked, already feeling a part of the family.

"Since five of our children left home this fall to attend Bible school or university, we felt we could take in five people. We heard of your need and decided that we wanted to help you find a new place to live," Mrs. Friesen explained.

Mr. Friesen handed the newcomers a list of the children's names and birthdates. It seemed almost irrelevant to the refugees at the moment because none of the twelve were around. Only the youngest four lived at home and they were asleep.

Mrs. Friesen served a night lunch of milk, apples, and cookies. "This milk smells peculiar," Anh whispered, turning up her nose. "I think its fresh farm milk and we're used to drinking canned milk," Phuong suggested.

Next came a tour of the house. "The girls may use this bedroom and the small bedroom upstairs. Nam, you will have to share the big bedroom upstairs with our youngest two sons, George and Sid," their hosts stated, giving them each a towel, wash cloth, and soap.

The girls slowly began to relax as they realized they had finally reached their destination. This would be home for the coming months. They could bathe and sleep in clean comfortable beds. They would not be cramped for space. Most of all they felt relieved to be in a home where there were loving parents who would look after their well-being during their adjustment to Canada.

After a brief get-acquainted session Mr. Friesen said, "We're going to bed now. Make yourselves at home. You may take baths and go to bed when you are ready."

By the time they had all showered, washed their hair (and run out of water), and were ready for bed it was three o'clock in the morning.

Phuong was the first of the five to awaken twelve hours later. Immediately she stepped to the window to look out. "Lan, look at the snow!" she shrieked with delight.

Lan jumped out of bed. "I have never seen a blanket of snow before," she whispered almost reverently. "It looks so white and soft. It feels strange. . . ." They stood by the window staring at the snow for a long time.

"We don't know how the snow feels and what it will do," Phuong said at last. "It's like our lives. We know where we are now, far away from home, but we don't know what life will be like from now on."

"I think we'll have a pleasant future," Lan stated simply.

Later that day Mr. Friesen explained the sponsorship policy to Nam and the girls and they discussed some future plans. Nam was frequently interrupted by the girls who wanted him to explain in Vietnamese what Mr. Friesen was saying.

"We as a family heard of the awful plight of your people and felt responsible to extend a helping hand," Mr. Friesen explained. "We are not of the wealthiest people in our country but we feel that we can help you get established so that you will eventually be able to make your own living.

"We have agreed to be responsible for your material well-being for one year. By then we hope you will be settled enough to make it on your own.

"We are willing to have you live in our house with us. This will be more economical than if you live by yourselves. We have a big house, big enough to share with others. This way you will also become familiar with the English language and our lifestyle more quickly."

Nam interjected, "All five of us are pleased about living with your family. We feel security in living with parents because we have always been taught to respect the elderly and we're used to having our parents make decisions for us."

"Job opportunities in this part of the country are scarce," Mr. Friesen continued. "Hopefully you can attend English language classes first which will assist you in finding jobs later.

"Your flights into Canada have been paid by the Canadian government. It is understood that you will each pay $675 within three years for the trip. You are not allowed to leave the country until that fee is paid. Neither may you become Canadian citizens until you have completely paid your flight.

"We want you to make yourselves at home in our house and be part of our family. Whenever you need anything or have a question about something please let us know. We encourage you to write letters to your relatives and hope that you will soon hear from them."

He showed them the miniature family mailbox. "This slot is where you place the letters you write. We'll take them to town to be posted. The other eleven slots are for the different family members. We'll let you use one of them." Mr. Friesen pointed to one of the cubicles. "Whenever any letters come for you we'll put them in here." Then he told them what address to use for their return address.

Writing letters was no chore. There was so much to write about and there were friends and relatives scattered all over the world.

"You girls sure talk a lot when you're upstairs by yourselves," remarked Nam one day. "How do you like living here?"

Thanh was first to answer. "I find it so strange to live in the country. I feel extremely isolated."

Lan agreed. "How will we ever meet other Vietnamese people? I always anticipated moving into a large city bustling with activity."

"It's quiet and peaceful but there are so few people — just isolated farms — and it makes me feel very lonely," Anh added.

"We can be thankful that we have each other at least and that we can share our feelings with each other," Phuong stated.

Communications between the Canadian and Vietnamese family members was difficult at the beginning and resulted in some embarrassing incidents.

The girls saw a waste basket beside the toilet and concluded that the toilet paper had to go in there after being used. Noticing the neatly folded patches of paper in the waste basket Mrs. Friesen wondered how she could explain to the girls that they should flush the used tissues down the toilet.

She took the girls into the washroom, put some of the folded papers into the toilet and flushed them away. "Always put paper in toilet," she said clearly.

"Yes,' responded the girls with polite smiles.

Mrs. Friesen soon learned that the girls always responded politely with a "yes" even when they did not understand her. Finally she decided to remove the waste basket from the washroom. That did the trick! The girls started flushing the tissues, but only until the garbage can was replaced.

Later Thanh explained, "We knew that normally the paper is flushed but because we saw the waste basket we thought there must be a problem with the toilet. So we put the paper in the waste basket."

Thanh found country life disappointing. "I just don't know what I'll do here with my life," she thought. "I'm afraid that any day I'll be asked to go and work in the barn. I'm afraid of cows. I couldn't dare touch one of them!" She and her sister had grown up in a wealthy home with servants and were not accustomed to doing their own housework, let alone tend animals.

"And oh, it's always so cold," she thought. "How much longer can I stand this? The lowest temperature we are used to from Vietnam is 16° C." These were concerns she constantly worried about and shared with the other girls.

For Nam the adjustment was less traumatic. The language was no problem for him. His sense of humor aided him in quickly establishing rapport with anyone he met. He felt useful because others relied on him to interpret.

When Nam was not around to help, the Friesen family and the girls spoke with gestures and isolated words. Constant repetition gradually improved the communication. Mrs. Friesen learned that Anh could knit so she gave her wool to make slippers. Anh also loved to cook and was frequently in the kitchen helping or preparing her own favorite Vietnamese dishes for the family.

* * *

The Friesens accepted the newcomers as their own family. In no time at all Jake and Mary Friesen had become "Mom" and "Dad" to the young refugees.

Dad Friesen knew what it was like to make a new beginning. Although he had grown up in Canada he had moved to Mexico to wed Mary, whose parents had emigrated there from Canada in 1948.

He and Mary farmed in Chihuahua, Mexico for seventeen

years until 1965 when they returned to Canada. Eventually they settled into dairy farming in Stratton, Ontario.

Jake was a hard-working, friendly man. He readily tried to learn some Vietnamese words and his warm outgoing manner quickly won the hearts of his new charges.

Both the elder Friesens were accepting, tolerant people. As a young wife Mary had suffered from epilepsy and was consequently occasionally forgetful. Her awareness of her own weakness seemed to have produced in her an amazing capacity to accept others non-judgmentally. She was quiet, and a woman of prayer.

Mom Friesen once related how well her temperamental spinner attachment for the washing machine worked when the Vietnamese girls did their laundry. She had tried to explain its foibles as best she could to them. "And then I went upstairs and prayed," she said. It worked fine.

Frequently the five newcomers sat together and discussed the different Friesen family members.

Nam found sixteen-year-old Sid amusing. "He doesn't say much," he said, "but I think he likes me. His face shows it. And he sure seems to do a great job of looking after the milking — thirty-eight cows morning and evening!"

George, two years older than Sid, was less talkative and his personality was more of a puzzle to Nam. "I wonder if those brothers ever talk to each other," he said. "When one comes into the room the other one leaves."

"I have the feeling they don't like us girls," Thanh commented. "They must think we're really strange or silly."

The sisters, Marilyn and Becky, were quite different from their brothers. The chattered and the house was filled with talk as soon as they came home from school.

"It's probably because they're younger," Nam concluded. "Once they reach their brothers' ages they'll become reserved too."

Becky, a grade three student, found it challenging to teach her new sisters and brother English. Lan told Nam, "We like it when Becky teaches us English. We don't feel inferior to her and she is a pleasant little sister to have around."

"She reminds me of my brother Jean because he's the same age," Nam said. "I wonder what life would be like if I had taken him along?"

Nam loved to tease Becky by saying her name in French, "Rébeka." Soon her classmates also started calling her Rébeka in a playful way.

Marilyn, barely a teenager, was not as lively as Becky but she had a sharp ear for phonics and frequently drilled the girls on their English pronunciations. And she also reminded her mother when her Low-German accent distorted her English.

A common trait of the Friesen family was to clear their throats rather noisily. Marilyn did this when washing up in preparation for bed. Frequently Nam teased, "Marilyn, are you starting your motor again?"

The second oldest son Phil, his wife Justina, and daughter Karen lived in the town of Stratton. Phil worked at the local meat processors and he and Justina were also active in church work.

Brothers Ray and Ike occasionally came home on weekends from Bible school in Steinbach, Manitoba.

"They always bring their sleeping bags and sleep on the floor in the living room or basement," Thanh noted to Nam. "I think we're in the bedrooms they used to have. I feel like we're intruding."

"I'm sure they don't mind," Nam consoled the girls. "Ray and Ike are quite different from their younger brothers. They seem pretty flexible. Being away from home and living in the city has probably helped them become more open. I really appreciate their openness and the times of fun we have when they come home."

Evelyn lived in Winnipeg and attended university, training to be a teacher. She visited home about once each month. "She always seems happy to meet us again," Lan said. "She enjoys helping us with our English and she always says we make a lot of progress with the language from one month to the next."

Lydia, the oldest in the family, lived with her husband Clifford and their two children, Mary Lois and Abram, on a farm at Barwick, thirteen kilometers from the parents.

Henry, the oldest son in the family, and his wife Mary with their children, Tammy and Travis, lived in Blumenort, Manitoba where Henry was a carpenter.

Then there were Betty and Wes, the youngest two of those away from home. They were also the farthest away. They attended the Peace River Bible institute in Sexsmith, Alberta.

"Mom Friesen said Betty and Wes are coming home for Christmas," Anh reminded the girls. "I wonder what they will be like."

14

"I'M BACK IN SCHOOL"

On their second day in Stratton Mr. Friesen took the new family members shopping in Rainy River. Nam bought a cheap watch and two post cards, one for his mother in Vietnam and one for Duyen. For Duyen he chose a card with a beautiful red rose on it.

"Duyen will love this card because she's very fond of flowers," he told Phuong.

Phil and Justina offered to have two of the girls at their home. The girls argued about who would go there.

"We all want to stay together so that we can talk to each other and feel more secure," Lan explained to Nam.

"Maybe Dad Friesen wants us to move out because we are too noisy," Thanh, always eager to please and afraid of inconveniencing their hosts, suggested. "Perhaps if we split up we'll put more effort into speaking English. I feel upset when the family speaks German, but maybe that's how they feel about listening to Vietnamese all the time."

Phuong declared, "I'm staying at Mom and Dad's because they are older and more mature. They are like parents to me."

Anh decided, "I'm the oldest of us girls so it's my responsibility to stay with Phuong. She needs extra care because of her health. If Phuong and I stay here she will be well taken care of and Nam will be close when Phuong needs him."

Reluctantly Lan and Thanh packed their belongings and moved to Phil and Justina's.

Nam did not stay in the house much. He found his way quickly into the community and soon he had requests to interpret for new refugee groups.

On November 14 Nam went to the immigration office in Fort Frances. To his surprise he met Kim and Tuan, a brother and sister whom he had learned to know well in the refugee camp. Kim and Tuan were sponsored by the Covenant Church in Rainy River and became welcome visitors in the Friesen residence.

The next day Dad Friesen took Nam and the girls to the neighboring farm to introduce them to a Vietnamese couple with twin baby boys who had arrived just a few days ago. The girls were delighted to meet other refugees from Vietnam and quickly made friends with them. Later they frequently stayed with this couple on weekends.

Sometimes Nam was invited to other homes to help resolve differences and misunderstandings between refugees and sponsors. Other times sponsors brought the refugees for whom they were responsible to meet Nam and discuss their needs.

One Saturday two Mennonite couples came to the Friesen farm with two young men their church had recently sponsored. The men refused to eat and did not respond to what was being done for them. Nam immediately went to the kitchen and prepared them each a strong cup of coffee with lots of sugar. They stayed for dinner with Nam sitting between them. He loaded (piled) their plates with rice, pork chops, and cooked carrots.

"Do they expect us to serve their food in their plates as you are doing?" inquired Mrs. Brubacher. "It looks like you have no problem getting them to eat."

"They say they don't like the way you cook the rice with milk. They don't like Canadian food," chuckled Nam. "They are also very lonesome for their relatives and would like to go to Toronto where they know some Vietnamese people."

Nam escorted them to their residence for the night to give further assistance.

The girls stayed at home most of the time and Dad Friesen became concerned about finding an opportunity for them to go to school. As the number of Asian immigrants in the area increased, the Manpower and Immigration office established classes in learning English as a second language both in Fort Frances and Rainy River.

So it was that on November 26, about a month after their arrival, Anh, Thanh, Lan, and Phuong started to attend school in Rainy River with five other immigrants. A bus picked them up at the driveway and took them the thirty-two kilometers to school.

"This reminds me of my first day of primary school — going into a new environment without my parents," reflected Lan, at the end of the first day. "It was quite easy today though. I enjoyed learning some Canadian customs."

"In Canada we greet each other in the morning by saying, 'Good Morning,' the teacher explained.

"When Mrs. Stamler said that in Canada we greet each other in the morning by saying 'Good Morning' I finally knew what Mom and Dad always say to us when we come for breakfast," Anh giggled. "I never knew what they meant." The girls had a good laugh over this.

When classes were dismissed the school bus picked them up. A kilometer before they got home the bus pulled on to the Catholic school yard, which was an unfamiliar place for the girls. The bus driver pointed to another bus on the yard. "See that bus? Please get into that bus now. That bus will take you home," he said.

The girls did not understand him. They were terrified and refused to get off. Old fears crept upon them. No, they would not follow the orders of a stranger. "We won't get off until the driver takes us home," Anh instructed the others.

The bus driver was at a loss to know what to do until he finally realized that Marilyn and Becky Friesen were on the other bus.

"Marilyn, can you tell your Vietnamese girls that they have to transfer to this bus? They don't seem to understand me."

Marilyn followed the driver to his bus and motioned the girls to come with her. When the girls saw her they burst into giggles, scurried off the bus, and followed Marilyn to the other vehicle.

Mom Friesen heard all six girls laughing heartily as they neared the house. "You must have had a good first day of school," she exclaimed. "What happened?" The girls could scarcely control themselves as they tried to explain. This episode drew mother and daughters closer together.

After that embarrassing experience the girls never minded transferring to another bus on their return from school.

"We aren't used to calling older people by their names. It feels strange to call you 'Mrs. Stamler'", Thanh said to her teacher, "In Vietnamese we would just say 'teacher.' It is also impolite to call older people by their first names. We don't even call an older brother or sister by their first name. We have a special word that we use for older people.

"We never say to our mother, 'please do this.' We say 'Mother please do this.' We find that Canadians don't show much respect to their older people," she continued.

Nam was curious to know about the girls' school experiences. "Do you enjoy it?" he asked.

"We love it," Phuong replied. "Our teacher takes us shopping and sometimes gives us clothes. She even invited us to her home a few times. She likes to have fun with us."

"She often talks to us about Canadian customs and tells us how we can find jobs," Anh reported. "She also wants us to talk about our traditions and encourages us to express our feelings."

"I'm glad you can go to school," he said. His voice was wistful as he added, "I hope to find a school soon too."

Nam recollected that the decision about his education had been made years ago in Vietnam. His parents wanted him to complete high school and get a university education. He recalled how disappointed his mother had been when he dropped out of school. Mr. Tran was more understanding because he too did not like the education system introduced under the new regime.

"But I knew that someday I'd go back to school to fulfill my parents' wishes," Nam thought. "I made a good start when I lived in the refugee camp."

When he came to Stratton, however, it was not as easy to enter school as he had anticipated. He was in a rural setting and there were no high schools close by. The church private school which the younger Friesens attended went only to grade eight.

"Surely I will find out about a school somewhere soon," he told himself.

With his background of high value placed on educational achievement, Nam found it strange that Dad Friesen did not encourage his children to finish high school. So far few of the Friesen children had completed high school, and Kathy was the only one that entered university. "Surely Sid must be interested in going to school because his intelligence level is so high," Nam thought, puzzled.

One evening Phil took Nam along to the Rainy River High School to play floor hockey with the church's youth. It was Nam's first exposure to a group of organized Canadian young people and he was amazed at their freedom. "They seem so friendly and free," he thought. "They drive thirty-two kilometers just to play hockey! To me it seems a waste of energy. In Vietnam we never dreamed of such freedom and luxury. We never even owned a car after 1975. But here people decide to go someplace and off they go. Nothing keeps them back."

On another day Mom and Dad Friesen took their five refugee children on a one-day trip to Steinbach, Manitoba, some 240 kilometers distance. On their way they encountered some difficulties when crossing the border into Minnesota enroute to Manitoba, so on their return they took the five-hour trip through Kenora rather than the three-hour trip through the United States. Again Nam marvelled at the freedom and efficiency possible in Canada. "In Vietnam it would take us all day to travel this distance," he said. "Here you travel back and forth in one day and still have time to do something in between."

It was on this trip that they visited the Steinbach Bible Institute where Ray and Ike studied. Jovial Ray gave Nam a tour of the campus which naturally included the library, Nam's greatest pleasure. Ray arranged for Nam to borrow some books on Ray's name. Once Nam got home he eagerly attacked the books, especially one on physics, a favorite subject of his.

A week later Nam had another opportunity to go to the immigration office in Fort Frances to interpret for some neighbors. He arrived at noon and the secretary told them they would have to wait an hour before the immigration officer returned.

While waiting Nam picked up a pamphlet on education through which he was referred to Mr. Ross, the local high school counselor. The secretary at the immigration office obligingly called Mr. Ross and made arrangements for Nam to see him at the school.

"I'll be back by one o'clock," Nam promised his friends and bounded out of the door with great expectations.

In his excitement he lost his way, however, and had to ask for directions.

When he found Mr. Ross, the counselor gave Nam a great deal of information and course outlines. "Study these and come back in about a week. Right now students are writing exams, but classes will resume in a week."

"What about transportation? I live in Stratton and don't have a vehicle." Nam knew that he could not afford to pay transportation costs.

"Don't worry about that," said Mr. Ross. "In our system transportation is provided for you free of charge. You get on the school bus at your driveway and it will bring you here."

"Really? I can't believe the freedom and opportunities here in Canada! Yes, I'll be back for classes when they start." Before Nam realized it, two hours had slipped by. He ran to the immigration office.

Chagrined, he learned that all the business had been looked after without him. The people he was to help were waiting for him.

"Did you want a ride back to Stratton?" joked Mr. Boersma.

"I feel terrible. I came along to interpret and then I just ran off. I am ashamed of myself, but yes, I would like a ride back!"

A week later Nam was enrolled at the Fort Frances High School. "I'm back in school after five years, and it's a strange feeling," mused Nam on the bus ride home. "Here I am, doing what my parents always wanted me to do. It's not school I like so much. But I'm so curious and my questions about the nature of physical life drives me to study. I want to learn things to satisfy my curiosity."

When Ray came home for the weekend he asked, "Well, Nam, how are the girls treating you in school? Are there nice girls there?"

"A lot of girls have asked me if my ring means that I'm married. I always say yes. That's an easy way to get rid of them," joked Nam.

"That's a good one," laughed Ray. "You can't let girls distract your studies like I'm being distracted by this charming girl named Inga in Bible school."

Nam had eight classes a day: four grade thirteen courses, two grade twelve courses, and two grade eleven courses. Keeping up with assignments was a constant struggle. He had been out of school so long and he had entered in the second term while all his classmates had been there since first term. He frequently borrowed notes from other students, sought help from willing and understanding teachers, and spent hours on his own trying to solve the problems.

In the midst of his busy schedule of studies Nam's

thoughts went frequently to Duyen. "Will she ever be able to escape Vietnam?" he wondered. The other question that bothered him was "how long should I wait until I tell the Friesens that I'm married?"

One day when the girls came home from their English classes they eagerly checked for mail as usual. Phuong exclaimed, "Mom, Nam has a letter from his wife!"

"But Nam isn't married," Mrs. Friesen protested. "It can't be from his wife."

"Yes, he is married. This letter is from his wife," Phuong insisted. She did not know that Nam had never spoken of Duyen to them.

Mrs. Friesen concluded that the girls did not know enough English to discuss the matter any further. "They probably don't know the proper meaning of 'wife' because they often refer to Kathy and Betty, who aren't married, as being good housewives," she told herself. "At any rate I'll ask Nam tonight to make sure."

"The girls told me that you had a letter from your wife," she said to Nam later. "Is it true that you're married?"

Nam responded with an abrupt "No." That settled the issue for Mrs. Friesen.

For Nam, however, it intensified his problem. "I can't tell them, not now that I've just denied my marriage another time," he thought miserably, "but sooner or later they'll find out. They'll probably be terribly upset with me when they discover the truth. They regard honesty so highly, and I can't let them down after all they've done for me."

Since he did not know how to unravel the misunderstanding that his registration as a single man and his subsequent silence had caused, he decided to do nothing and tried to put it out of his mind.

One problem that Nam dealt with more decisively, however, was his smoking habit. Although money was scarce, Nam had always managed to obtain another package of cigarettes somehow. He had soon realized that smoking was not acceptable in the Friesen family. He resorted to smoking in his room with the window open. "That should be okay," he reasoned.

George began to smoke in the bedroom too. Nam realized that his roommate could hide his smoking by doing it with Nam, for the family would attribute the smell of cigarette smoke to Nam's habit.

Mr. Friesen, hesitant to confront Nam directly, finally approached him with an offer. "We would really appreciate it if you didn't smoke in the house, Nam," he said. "I'll give you a dollar a day for not smoking in the house."

Nam was not sure what to think about the suggestion. "If Dad really wants me to quit, why doesn't he just come out and say so, and I'll stop! Does he think I'll find it hard to quit and so tries to motivate me with money?"

To Mr. Friesen he said, "Okay Dad, I'll finish this package and then I'll quit."

Nam surprised even himself by indeed ceasing to smoke altogether after the package was finished. "This is a miracle," he thought. "Dad must really be praying hard for me!"

15

"THEIR GOD MUST HAVE TOLD THEM TO SPONSOR US"

One December Saturday evening, Ray, Evelyn and Nam sat around the dining room table until late at night discussing various issues in their usual brother-to-sister manner. The conversation naturally drifted to Ray's irresistible attraction for Inga and his interest in marrying her.

Nam voiced strongly his opinions about the responsibilities of marriage. "I was once madly in love with a girl too. Since then I've realized I'm not ready for marriage. I wouldn't be able to support a wife and children. I can't even support myself.

"Here in Canada it seems easy for young people to get married, because it is so easy to make a living. In Vietnam the pressures are so great from all sides that you don't enter into marriage light-heartedly."

With Christmas approaching, excitement in the Friesen home increased. Mom Friesen baked dozens of Christmas cookies. Kathy was sewing and helping with other Christmas preparations.

One Saturday Nam and Phuong helped Kathy make a banner with the inscription "Jesus is the Light of the World" which they placed outside above the garage doors. It was illuminated by a string of purple Christmas lights.

On December 21, Betty and Wes returned from Bible school in Sexsmith, Alberta. They had never met Nam and the girls but had heard much about them. Betty and Wes were glad to meet them as well as to be reunited with their family. Ray and Ike also came home for the Christmas break. Suddenly the house was full of people; it buzzed with activity and exchanges of news and happenings over the last months. Everyone had so much to say.

After a while Becky noticed that Phuong and Anh were not downstairs with the rest of the family. She went to their bedroom. An unexpected scene met her eyes. Both girls were sitting in bed, their faces wet with tears. She had never seen them cry, and it touched and concerned her.

Becky found her mother busy preparing supper in the kitchen. She tugged at her arm. "Ahn and Phuong are just sitting in their room crying, Mom," she said.

"Oh dear, I've neglected those girls in my excitement over having everyone else come home. They must be homesick, seeing us so excited about having Betty and Wes come home and they're far from their homes, not knowing if they'll ever see their families again." Mrs. Friesen quickly went upstairs.

As only a mother can, she lovingly put her arms around the girls' shoulders and let them know that she cared and tried to understand. The girls did not say much but Mrs. Friesen sensed their deep hurt and loneliness.

Sunday was the day of the family Christmas gathering. Everyone came home, making a total of twenty-six people including the five Vietnamese young people. The kitchen buzzed with activity as all helped to prepare the festive meal they would enjoy together.

Everyone participated in a service at the church and then returned for the Christmas dinner. The tables were simply but bountifully spread with tasty food: turkey with bread stuffing, mashed potatoes, rice, peas and carrots, tossed green salad, fruit salad, and jello salad. Dessert was the usual Christmas offering of lemon meringue or blueberry pie.

Pleasant conversation and laughter drifted from one end of the long table to the other while everyone heartily enjoyed the meal.

After the meal was finished and the dishes were done the whole family assembled in the living room for the Christmas program.

This year Becky and Mom had planned the program, consisting of carols, special musical presentations, games, poems, a Bible quiz on the Christmas story, and reminiscing of Christmases in the past.

Nam shared of some of their experiences to familarize Betty and Wes with their history. "About ten months ago I was in prison in Vietnam," he said. "The Lord rescued me from prison in a miraculous way. When the warden examined me I told him that I never intended to escape Vietnam but my friend had forced me to accompany him. I told him that I was on the side of communism. I was released, but as soon as I came home I set my mind to attempting another escape. I hadn't planned to lie to the warden; it seemed at that point that that was God's way of setting me free."

Phuong, Lan, Anh, and Thanh sang several songs in Vietnamese and Nam translated them into English.

Dad Friesen told the Christmas story as found in the Bible, explaining that God sent his son Jesus to the world to be born as a baby.

"At Christmas we celebrate the birth of Jesus Christ. We don't want to remember only his birth but think about the reason why he came," he said. "Jesus came to the earth to save us sinful people from being punished eternally for our sins. Jesus grew up, lived among the people of his day, and taught them numerous principles about how to live. He also performed many wonders and miracles, but in the end the people became angry with him and nailed him to the cross.

"Jesus would have had the power to escape, but he loved us so much that he was willing to die on the cross to pay for our sins. Because Jesus paid for our sins we can know that when we die we will go to heaven and live with him for eternity. Everyone who admits that he has sin in his life, confesses these sins to God, and believes that Jesus paid for them when he died on the cross can have the assurance of life everlasting after death.

"Because Jesus did so much for us in giving his own life for us, we have a custom of exchanging gifts at Christmas time. These gifts show our love for each other. They are just small tokens compared to God's love for us."

Mom and Dad Friesen handed their gifts to the children. Each of their Vietnamese children received a watch. Then the children distributed their gifts to each other and the parents. Following this everyone had a turn at showing their gifts and saying thank you. The gifts ranged from practical kitchen aids and mechanical tools to games and story books.

Mom Friesen served a "faspa" (evening lunch) of a variety of cookies, cheeses, pickles, apple cider, coffee, fresh brown bread and butter, and Christmas fruit cake. This, following the oranges, peanuts, chocolates, and candy they had been munching during the gift exchange left all feeling thoroughly stuffed and well fed.

The evening was spent around the table playing various games such as Master Mind, Dutch Blitz, Racko, Probe and Clue.

Hearing the carols throughout the Christmas season had a nostalgic effect on Nam. Instead of peace and happiness he felt tears welling up. "How can I be happy when on the other side of the earth many of my people are suffering, thousands are waiting in refugee camps, and countless numbers of children and wives are longing for the presence of their fathers and husbands?"

These thoughts led him to memories of his family and past Christmases when they had hoped for a better future, and made the season initially depressing instead of joyful. Then he realized, "Worrying over these things won't improve the situation. I've got to put these thoughts aside and live in my new environment."

Nam committed his hopes and desires into God's hands

and as a result started to appreciate Christmas in a new way. He realized that he needed the spiritual strength which only God could give him.

During the rest of the Christmas holidays the family often played table games or worked on a 1500-piece jigsaw puzzle. A bowl of peanuts and oranges usually stood on the table. Interspersed with games and eating were joking, teasing, and serious conversations.

Nam's favorite game was Master Mind. While calculating the solutions he would often twist his narrow gold wedding ring.

"Does your ring represent something special, Nam?" inquired Betty.

"Yes, it does. See this D? That's for my girlfriend. Her name begins with D."

"What is her name?"

"Duyen."

"Don't you miss her a lot?"

"Yes, I do. I miss her very much. When I awake in the morning the first thing I see is this ring with the D facing me like this. It always reminds me of her," Nam answered solemnly.

Nam frequently thought about Duyen and Bao in Vietnam. He did not allow himself to become melancholy, however. He always seemed to have some joke up his sleeves and his good sense of humor often helped relieve tension in the family.

Phuong and Anh were more timid than Nam and spent much time alone together or visiting other Vietnamese friends after school or on weekends.

Phil and Justina had a shortage of water so Lan and Thanh usually came to the elder Friesens' place on Saturdays to do their laundry, take baths, and wash their hair. Often the girls took the sewing machine and iron upstairs and congregated in their room, chattering and sewing.

On New Year's Eve the church youth met at Friesens' for a "watch-night" service and a celebration of Nam's birthday.

About twenty young people gathered, spending the evening playing large group games in which everyone gladly participated. Roars of laughter indicated that all were having a good time. After the games Nam cut his cake and served everyone around the circle.

At 11:30 p.m. the whole party trooped outside to see in the New Year. Everyone joined hands to form a circle under the beautiful winter sky.

A number of young people shared what God had meant to them in the past year. Others voiced their concerns and prayer requests for the coming year. Between testimonies Ike led the group in songs and choruses of praise to God.

Nam was awed. "You people have a lot to be thankful for. Here I am enjoying this freedom with you when my family is in Communist Vietnam suffering. In Vietnam we could never dream of gathering like this to worship God. We just don't have that freedom. We must remember to be thankful for this. Remember those who can't experience this."

Hearts became quiet before God as Ray counted down the last thirty seconds of the year 1979. Only God knew what the new year would hold for each one in the circle, but everyone was assured that God held their future and would go with them. Several people led the group in prayer, thanking God for his blessings in the past year and asking for guidance in 1980.

After a friendly snowball fight all returned to their respective homes.

"Attending church regularly is a new experience for us," Thanh said to Mom and Evelyn. The Friesen family always attended the Sunday morning worship service and Sunday school as well as Thursday night's family Bible study and hymn singing.

"Anh, Lan, and I are Buddhist; we had never been in a church before we came to Stratton. We went to a Catholic school in Vietnam. That's why we thought that all churches had statues, crosses, candles, and flowers. Your small Mennonite church is different."

"We don't like to go to church," Anh explained once when the girls visited with Evelyn. "We can't understand what the man says. He talks too fast. Often he talks German. I'm scared to go to Sunday school. Everyone has to read a Bible verse and people laugh when I say the words in French. Some people talk to us after church, but I'm much too afraid to speak English so I don't say anything. They will laugh when I speak incorrectly."

Since Mr. Friesen was the chairman of the church executive the family usually stayed at church until everyone else was gone. For the Vietnamese it seemed an almost endless time of waiting and trying to avoid questions from the church people.

"I didn't care to go to church either," Thanh shared. "I often wondered why your family sponsored us. Then I thought 'the whole family goes to church, so their God must have told them to sponsor us. This family is really nice to us, so I will go to church to please them.' You know Kathy, our parents never taught us to go to church."

Lan said, "At first I felt upset and inferior when people in church talked to me. I couldn't understand them and I couldn't talk back to them. Most Canadians talk too fast. That makes me nervous. Then it is very difficult to understand them."

"At first we girls often laughed throughout the church service," Thanh remembered. "Everything seemed so strange to us. We thought the preaching was no good because we couldn't understand a word of it. It sounded so funny to hear everyone talking in a different language."

"Phuong, how did you like church?" Evelyn asked.

"For me it wasn't so strange because I was used to attending church. I attended a Catholic church in Vietnam. I love to sing and I learned to enjoy the messages in your church."

One Saturday evening Mr. and Mrs. Friesen took Nam and Phuong to the neighboring Catholic church. Phuong's spirits revived the minute she entered the church. This felt like home to her. Her heart had longed for that with which she was familiar. Excitedly she told Mom Friesen what the various images represented. After that she attended Mass regularly on Saturday nights and went to church with the Friesens on Sunday. In a few months, however, she tired of it and dropped the Saturday service.

Phuong treasured the Bible which she received from the Friesens. She would read in it often with her Vietnamese-English dictionary and notebook beside her.

The exposure to Christianity caused Nam to do some serious thinking. "I realize that my approach to Christianity differs from that of the Christians at Stratton," he reflected. "They believe in Jesus Christ as their personal Saviour from sin and this belief is very much a part of their everyday lives. I believe in God too, but I can't change so quickly and believe like they do. For them it seems so simple. The whole family is together and they all believe alike. They only need to practice some self-discipline, but have nothing to worry about.

"I came to Canada with certain goals and religion was not one of them," Nam admitted. "I'm living for my family and my aim is to help them. I must first assist them before I can focus on myself, so I don't think I can change my beliefs. I've noticed that Canadians aren't as loyal and committed to their families as we Vietnamese are."

One winter evening Nam accompanied part of the family to an evangelistic crusade in International Falls, Minnesota. Nam summed up the message: "The evangelist talks about how to live the everyday life and how to treat one's fellow-man. He talks about humility versus pride and how pride is a sin causing people to do harmful things. What this man says is true and applies to everyone regardless of their religious or political background. I know that there's a lot of pride in my life which I need to get rid of."

When the evangelist gave a call for those who needed assurance of salvation to come forward Nam could not resist. The message had gripped his heart and he decided to humble himself and ask God for forgiveness.

After this experience Nam still struggled. "I always feel

sorry for others, especially my family in Vietnam, and I can't do anything to turn them down. I must help my family before I can think of changing my own beliefs.''

16

"WE WANT TO THANK YOU"

Nam frequently spent nights in Fort Frances with friends, also recent refugees, while attending high school there. The refugees were grateful for what their sponsors were doing for them. Someone came up with the idea of celebrating TÊT, the Vietnamese New Year, by putting on a banquet in honor of their sponsors. This idea spread like fire and a committee was formed to plan the party for February 16.

Money was the biggest obstacle because very few of them had jobs. Most of the Vietnamese and Chinese refugees were in language school or just starting to earn money. When other organizations heard of the need they offered their support. The Lions Club of Fort Frances donated $450 and the Presbyterian Church offered the use of their church basement.

Various committees were elected to be in charge of the meal, decorating, invitations, and the program. The decorating committee covered bare tree branches with yellow crepe paper flowers for table centers. A larger tree was decorated the same way and graced the stage.

When the guests arrived they received welcoming handshakes from hosts standing along the walls in the hallway and the lobby. Then the 300 visitors feasted on the Vietnamese-

Chinese banquet, served by the hostesses, starting with vegetable, rice, and noodle soup. The main course consisted of "Chā go", rolled rice paper filled with ground pork, pepper, salt, fish sauce, carrots, crabs, onions, and garlic. These rolls were deep-fried and dipped in various fish sauces. Then there was pork stew with boiled eggs.

Nam, the chairman of the celebration, introduced each new dish by explaining its ingredients and how it was made.

"I enjoy the reaction to my explanations," Nam chuckled to himself. "But it sounds like they're getting anxious for something to wash down the spices which practically burn their mouths. I better check with the kitchen staff about the coffee situation."

"The coffee isn't ready," Anh informed him. "They'll have to wait a few more minutes."

He returned to the microphone to console the destitute guests. "I know some of you are anxiously waiting for coffee. Our custom is to drink only at the end of the meal and since this is a Vietnamese meal you won't get anything to drink until the end. So this time you'll just have to adjust to our tradition. If you find that difficult then hopefully it will help you understand how some of us sometimes feel about fitting into your culture!

"For dessert we will serve a sweet jellied drink called Ché đâu zanh. This consists of dried yellow peas well-cooked with sugar, vanilla and coconut milk. After the dessert you will get your coffee."

After the meal the Vietnamese Refugee Group presented a program consisting mostly of songs. Anh sang a number of solos. The students of the Rainy River Language School of which Anh, Thanh, Lan, and Phuong were a part, sang. Nam translated the meaning of these songs into English. Nature was one of the prevailing themes.

Those of the Friesen family who attended sang Nam's favorite Canadian song, which he had learned in church, "I'm so Glad I'm a Part of the Family of God."

Nam explained TÊT NGUYÊN DÁN to the guests. "TÊT is

the Vietnamese New Year's celebration. Our New Year's day is timed according to the moon calendar. Because Vietnam is an oriental country our celebration is related to our culture and religion. Most people don't have any religion except for remembering their ancestors. For this reason we celebrate the memory of our ancestors on TÊT."

Small gifts of appreciation were given to the sponsors. The small children received a dollar bill in a tiny shiny red envelope. Tickets were handed out to everyone. Ten tickets had numbers on them, ranging from one to ten, and the other tickets were blank. Whoever was lucky enough to receive a numbered ticket received a small gift package with a bar of soap, toothpaste, or other practical items.

The sponsors found the evening enjoyable and enlightening. "It helps us understand the culture shock our new citizens must experience when they have to eat strange food and are bombarded from all sides with a strange language," said one.

At the door each guest received a twig from the New Year's tree, many good wishes, and good-bye handshakes from the men. The women were in the kitchen cleaning up.

17

"I HAVE A CONFESSION TO MAKE"

Early in 1980 Nam received a letter from his aunt and uncle in the U.S.A. It informed him that Duyen was in Singapore.

He could scarcely comprehend the news. "It's a miracle!" he thought. "I didn't know if I'd ever see her again. What a brave girl, to escape on her own."

Nam learned that Duyen left just four or five months after he did, about the time he arrived in Canada. But he knew no details. How had she managed to escape? Was Bao with her? What about her father?

In Duyen's first letter from Singapore she explained how she escaped:

> When my father heard that you left, he insisted that my sister Huyen and I follow you. He claims he'll manage on his own, and does not want to impose on anyone. We didn't take Bao with us. Your mother promised to take care of him. I know she will take good care of him too.
>
> I left Vietnam hoping to meet you again, but a few times I wondered if I would. We were forty-nine people on a small boat leaving Saigon. Soon our boat was shipwrecked. We were lucky to be rescued by a Holland merchant ship. This ship was on its way to Vietnam to deliver some food. For two

days we stayed in the bottom compartment of the ship, not daring to move or make any noise lest we be discovered by communist guards. All we could do was pray for protection.

Later we had to be taken to Sinagpore to be registered as refugees, so that's how I got here. Holland will accept all of us into their country if we want to go.

Nam responded with:

I was surprised to hear that you made a safe escape. How did you manage to make arrangements? When I left there seemed to be no solution to the problem.

Duyen, I want you to come to Canada but there's a minor problem involved. When I left Vietnam I never took along our marriage certificate. In fact I never even got one. Remember after we were married circumstances were so unsettling that I never got around to going to the registration office to pick it up?

When I applied for sponsorship I registered as single. At the time I planned to change my marital status as soon as I'd come to Canada. When I got here I decided not to cause a disturbance right away. I decided to wait until you could send me a copy of our marriage certificate.

A few days later when Nam came home from school Dad Friesen told him there had been a call from the United States requesting help for his wife.

"What's this all about?" he asked. "The lady was very persistent, demanding help for your wife. I told her you weren't married. She became angry and insisted you are married. She says your wife is in Singapore waiting to be sponsored. She also claimed to be related to your wife."

"You must be joking! I'm not even married!" Nam attempted to laugh it off.

"No Nam, I'm not joking. Are you married?"

"No, I'm not." Nam lied. "They must have mixed me up with someone else. How could anyone come up with such a story?"

Alone, Nam felt miserable. "How can I confuse Dad enough to make him drop the issue? If only my relatives would keep quiet about this I would be able to straighten it out eventually. But sooner or later I won't be able to cover up anymore and then what will happen to my reputation?"

During evening chores Dad brought up the subject again. This time Nam started to give in a little. "Well, Dad," he said, "I was engaged to her, but we never married."

"I hope that answer will satisfy Dad," Nam thought. "But he looks upset. I know I've failed to convince him. Perhaps I'll have to confess the truth."

That night Nam agonized, searching for a way out of his dilemma. Finally he decided to tell the truth about his marriage. "Lying must be a pattern with me by now," he realized in horror. "Maybe I lied so much when I was young and now I'm suffering the results of it. I can't stand this any longer. I'm going downstairs to talk to Dad."

Like a penitent son he trudged downstairs and found Mr. Friesen sitting at his desk reading the Bible.

"Dad, may I talk to you?"

"Yes, Nam, of course."

"Well, Dad you know that phone call — I — I — I am married." He went on to tall Dad Friesen about Duyen, why he escaped without her, and why he registered as a single man.

Dad's reaction surprised Nam. "I can't believe it!" he thought. "I figured Dad would be mad at me but instead, he prayed for me. He committed Duyen and the whole situation into God's hands. What a relief!"

"Now that you've told me, do you want to tell the rest of the family or would you rather that I tell them?" Dad asked.

Nam turned this over in his mind. "Isn't it enough that I've told Dad?" he struggled. "Does everyone have to know? Why is this such a big issue with Dad? But if I don't tell them I'm sure Dad will. He believes in honesty."

"Since I'm the one who made up the story, Dad," he said, "I'll have to be the one to tell them the truth about it."

"How about telling the family tomorrow at supper?" Dad suggested.

"Okay Dad."

The next day Nam mulled the matter over constantly. "Do they really have to know? Now that I've deceived them once will they ever trust me again? I feel terrible about it. They'll think I'm a horrible person. So far they've liked me, but now? Is there no way of getting out of this?"

At supper Dad announced. "Nam has something he wants to tell the family."

"I have a confession to make to all of you," Nam said slowly. "I am married. My wife has escaped Vietnam and is at a refugee camp now."

Everyone's jaw dropped. "Nam — married? Is it possible? He's been such a super brother and now this? Who is he anyway? We thought we knew him," were the unspoken reactions. The rest of the meal was exceptionally quiet.

The confession also brought into the open the tension between the two "brothers" of such vastly different backgrounds. Together in their upstairs rooms after supper, Nam felt a strong negative reaction from George. "I don't think George ever liked me and now I know for sure that he hates me. He's getting mad at me, I can feel it," he thought.

"That's all right George," Nam said, trying to pacify his roommate, "I know you're angry. You need to express your feelings. I know you can't understand why I did this."

"I don't care if I understand you or not, I don't want to see you in this house anymore!" George kicked Nam's chair.

Nam took a deep breath and said, "You must be hurt and probably think that since I've told one lie I could have told more. And that could be possible."

George kept on kicking Nam's chair. Nam stood, his anger rising too. "What do you want, George?"

"I don't want to see you in this house anymore!" George repeated.

"Okay, no problem." Nam said casually, though he felt hurt and depressed.

Once more Nam sought out Dad Friesen. "Dad, George is mad at me. He tells me to leave this house. I don't think I can put up with him any longer either. I'm leaving and will manage on my own somehow."

Dad was sorry to hear about the dispute. "I know that you must really hurt. I'll talk to George and see if we can't work it out."

"Dad, I think it's all right for George to react like this, just as much as it was right for me to do what I did."

It was decided that for the good of everyone involved the girls would give up the bedroom downstairs and share the upstairs bedroom so that Nam could have his own room.

"Now about your wife, Nam. Would you be interested in having the church sponsor her?" Dad offered.

"No, that's all right," Nam said immediately. "She's my responsibility and I'll manage somehow, sometime. Maybe she can go to the U.S.A. first and then we can get together later."

When Duyen found out that Nam had registered as a single man and lied to his sponsors about his marriage she became very angry. "If he denied the fact that he was married, I guess he doesn't really love me," she decided. "I don't care if I ever see him again. I left Vietnam hoping to meet him and live with him as a married couple should but now nothing matters. I don't care where I go. I might as well go to Holland or to the U.S.A. and live with my older sister."

In Duyen's next letter to Nam she wrote:

> Can you imagine how I felt when I heard that you entered Canada under the pretense of being single? I used to think you were sorry to leave me behind but now I know you just pretended to love me. You've been deceiving me all this time.
>
> Now I know why I never received a single letter from you while I was still in Vietnam. Your mother got a number of letters and post cards from you but I never received any. I used to blame the postal service for this because I expected you to write.
>
> Do you not care at all about my feelings? Am I nobody? Did you actually leave Vietnam just to get away from me? Don't you care that you have a son and wife to support? You've disgraced your whole family by being untrue to your wife.

All these months I desperately longed to see you again. Now I wish I had been drowned in the sea. What's left in life for me? You obviously don't want me. My baby is still in Vietnam and will manage all right without me. Why should I keep on living?

I can always go and live with my sister in Kansas. Since we were rescued by a Dutch ship, Holland is responsible for us. I might as well go to Holland and forget that I ever knew you.

For all I know you're contemplating marriage with some Canadian girl in an attempt to start a new life without me.

Your one-time happy wife,
Duyen

"Why did things have to turn out this way?" Nam's heart cried in anguish as he stared at Duyen's angry letter. "I never meant to hurt her. I did what seemed logical at the time. I ended up deceiving the Friesen family and what's worse, I've lost Duyen's confidence in me. Why is this happening when my intentions were unselfish?

"How will I ever convince Duyen that I still love her? How can I possibly make her understand? I've created this mess so I'm responsible to get myself out of it. I want to sponsor Duyen but I don't have enough money. And before I can earn a lot of money I need more education. All this takes time. Will Duyen ever be able to understand that?

"God, I've messed things up so badly. Have mercy on me," was Nam's constant prayer that night as he tossed and turned, seeking a way out of his predicament.

In the days to come Dad Friesen insisted that the church should get involved and offered again to sponsor Duyen.

Nam's response was, "I'll have to wait and see what will happen. Maybe she will go to Holland." He found it humiliating to accept help in an area that was his responsibility.

Nam moved in with friends in Fort Frances. "This way I might be able to find a part-time job and start helping my wife," he told Dad Friesen.

He searched for jobs but found nothing. Letters from Duyen became more frequent, constantly accusing him of not caring about her. Nam became more withdrawn and tense each day. He appeared to be busy studying, but most of his time was spent worrying about how he would handle everything. "My wife needs help, my family needs help, I need to get an education, and I can't find a job. . . ."

Finally Dad Friesen offered to pay Nam for helping with the chores if he would move home again. Nam graciously accepted this offer and started doing chores before and after school as well as helping on the farm on weekends.

When Evelyn came home for the weekends she noticed that Nam was not the same person. She missed the conversations and times of fun they had had together. Now he always appeared to be busy studying, spending most of his spare time in his room with the door closed.

One afternoon Evelyn decided to disturb him.

"Hi, Nam! Are you studying?"

"Yes. I have an English essay to finish by next Thursday and I can't seem to get the words together."

"How is school going for you?" Evelyn asked.

"It's not going for me!" Nam said with a grin. "Do you want to see my first report card?"

"Sure."

Nam handed her the report card.

"You have a lot of B's," Evelyn observed. "That's terrific. It doesn't seem like you're having too much difficulty, considering that this is your first time in a Canadian school and you have the language to cope with too."

"If I had only school to think of, life would be easy. I have so many other worries."

"Like?"

"Well, as you know, I have a wife. I don't know what will happen to her. I'm responsible for her but I don't know how I can help her. Maybe she'll have to go live with her sister in the U.S. for a while first. These concerns often keep me from concentrating on my studies. During the night I always worry about the future," Nam shared.

"How's Duyen making out in the refugee camp?" Evelyn wondered.

"She's doing all right, — I guess." Nam faltered. "But," he thought to himself, "That's not true. She isn't doing all right. She's angry at me. She's hurt. Now she doesn't want to see me again and this family may never meet her. Should I tell Evelyn how Duyen feels? No, I can't. It's my problem and I'll just have to learn to live with it."

"Do you have any idea how long it might take until Duyen will come to Canada?" Evelyn broke the silence.

"No, I don't. Before she can come I'll have to change my marital status at the immigration office," Nam said.

"Is that quite complicated?"

"I don't think so." Nam hesitated. "Dad found out that we have a year to change any false information on our Canadian registration."

"It must be a rough struggle for you, Nam. I'm praying for you and Duyen and believe that somehow things will fall into place at the right time. Remember that we as a family love you and want to help you in any way we can."

Later Evelyn asked Mom, "Is Nam always this quiet and withdrawn? It's so strange not to have him full of jokes like he was at first."

"He's become very quiet," Mom said her voice full of concern. "It seems that he feels remorse for having deceived us. He does his chores well and eats with us but the rest of the time at home he spends in his room with the door closed. He says he's studying, but I think he has a lot on his mind that he's trying to sort through. I believe it's very important that we pray for him.

"We've suggested a number of times that the church will sponsor Duyen," Mom continued, "but he doesn't accept the offer. It seems he thinks he has to wait until he can do it himself."

Duyen persistently resisted Nam in her letters. Nam finally decided to give up. "She'll never believe me, so why continue apologizing?" he reasoned. "If I really am what she accuses me of, unfaithful to her, then why bother writing her? I'll write her one more letter. Then I'll forget about her because that's what she claims I've done."

Nam wrote:

Duyen, the choice is yours. I feel responsible to work with you in trying to get Bao out of Vietnam and live with us here in Canada. If you don't believe me, it's your choice. I'm not going to try to convince you forever that I always cared for you.

I believe if I was in your shoes I would react the same way you've been reacting to me. I take the blame for all the turmoil you've gone through. If you still want to turn your back on me by never coming to Canada I will understand.

This final letter softened Duyen's heart. When Nam's letters ceased, she realized that she had been too critical of him and decided to once more respond to his love.

She went to the Canadian delegation office and applied to join her husband in Stratton, Ontario. Checking their records the delegates said, "You have no husband in Stratton. Our records offer no proof of what you told us."

Quickly Duyen ran back to her shelter, gathered all the letters she had received from Nam since she came to Singapore and brought them to the office. "Here is proof that I have a husband in Stratton. Look at these letters. Look at the Canadian postage stamps. See the Stratton post mark and Nam's return address. If you don't believe me, read these letters."

The letters were sufficient evidence for the delegates to begin to process her application. Meanwhile Nam worked toward changing his marital status on his immigration document.

Now that Nam knew that Duyen was willing to come to Canada he decided to seek help with sponsoring Duyen. Dad Friesen filed a request to sponsor her, knowing that it would take a number of months to process the application.

Nam finished school in early April, 1980, and worked for

the Ministry of Natural Resources on a deer survey for several weeks. He earned about three hundred dollars which he proudly put into a savings account.

At that point Nam felt more positive about his situation. "I must say life is getting easier," he thought. "Duyen and I will see each other again. I've been able to earn some money for the time when she comes to Canada. Come to think of it, even George has become more tolerant of me. I think he's finally starting to like me too."

18

"WE'RE BECOMING INDEPENDENT"

Nam discussed his responsibility towards his sister and cousins with Dad. "The girls will be finished with language school in the beginning of May and hope to get jobs after that. They want to move to a city where there will be more job opportunities and better chances to continue their education while working. Their first choice is Toronto because they already have friends there."

Dad advised, "I suggest they move to Winnipeg. Winnipeg is only about 320 kilometers from here, whereas Toronto is more like 1800 kilometers. If they move to Winnipeg Kathy will be able to help them get jobs and get settled. Since Winnipeg is closer we can also take them there rather than paying for transportation to Toronto. It will also be easier to keep in contact and we'll be more readily available to assist if they should ever need some help."

The girls and Nam decided that it would be best to move to Winnipeg for the time being. They could move to Toronto later on if they wished. At the end of April, Mr. and Mrs. Friesen drove to Winnipeg and together with Evelyn investigated job opportunities and looked for a place to live.

The house next to Evelyn's place, which was owned by the same person, turned out to be the most appropriate location.

The rent was reasonable and the landlady very interested in helping refugees.

On May 8, their last day of school, the girls came home from school saddened because they were going to miss their much-loved and appreciated teacher, Mrs. Stamler.

That evening everyone went to church for the regular Thursday night family meeting. After church Phil and Justina brought Thanh and Lan over with all their possessions.

The four girls placed their belongings on the dining room table and began packing their boxes. Mom Friesen added some dishes and utensils she did not need and prepared several boxes of canned goods.

It was late by the time everything was packed and the girls were ready for bed. They looked forward to earning their own money and managing on their own but at the same time they dreaded moving away from Mom and Dad Friesen's home and care, to fend for themselves.

Thanh especially felt insecure about moving. "I'm afraid I'll get lost in the city," she confided to Mom Friesen. "Everything will be new again. I'm afraid to talk to strangers. They may laugh at my poor English."

The next morning Mr. Friesen packed some frozen meat and loaded all the boxes into the back of the station wagon. Kim, a Vietnamese girlfriend from Rainy River, moved with them so, with Mom and Dad, they were seven people in the station wagon as well as all the luggage.

They had to take the six-hour route around Kenora, Ontario because the girls could not legally pass through the State of Minnesota.

It was refreshing to get out of the car when they arrived at their destination in Winnipeg. Their three-bedroom main floor suite was furnished with the basic furniture. The girls carried in their boxes and gradually planned who would have which bedroom and how they would arrange their belongings.

Mr. Friesen took the girls grocery shopping, leaving them with a good supply of groceries, and paid one month's rent.

Jobs were also all ready arranged for them and they would start work on Monday. They would be all right now until they would get their first paycheck in two weeks.

Betty had come to the city earlier in the week to live with Evelyn for the summer. Together they prepared a supper for the group and then Betty accompanied her parents back to Stratton for the weekend.

On Saturday the girls were busy unpacking and settling in. Evelyn showed them where to catch buses and how to get to work on Monday. The cold and drizzly weather made their first Saturday a miserable day, however.

Sunday the weather was no better, but the girls came along to church with Evelyn.

"After waiting in the cold drizzle for a bus, transferring buses and then walking several blocks I've decided I won't do this again," Anh told the other girls. "To me church just isn't worth that much effort."

"Does it always rain in Winnipeg?" Lan asked Evelyn.

"No. I don't think Winnipeg gets any more rain than Stratton does," Evelyn answered. But the girls seemed to doubt her.

"I didn't know Winnipeg was so cold," Anh complained. "I don't think I will like living here."

They had lunch at Evelyn's place and then went home. Immediately they turned the thermostat up to 28° C to warm up for a change.

"I'm convinced that Winnipeg will always be cold and drizzly. I regret that I ever agreed to move here," Phuong muttered. "I want to move to a place where the weather will be like Vietnam's."

On Monday all the girls except Thanh went to work. They encountered countless small frustrations. That evening they shared them, laughed heartily over foolish mistakes they had made and helped each other with the English jargon of the sewing factory which they had heard and remembered.

Tuesday was a much better day because they knew what to expect.

On Tuesday afternoon Evelyn took Thanh to an optometrist. While walking Thanh shared her concerns with Evelyn. "I'm scared to speak to strangers. Evelyn, I don't think I will ever marry. You know why? I'm afraid to speak to Canadian boys."

"What do you mean? I'm always surprised at how well you speak English," Evelyn said encouragingly. "You are so concerned about using the correct grammatical forms that soon you'll speak English better than I do."

In the days to come Thanh frequently came to ask Evelyn for definitions of words and phrases she had picked up. She wanted to know the proper usage of certain words and make sure her sentence structure was correct.

"We're going to school at the International Centre," Lan informed Evelyn one evening.

"Who told you about this school?"

"A Chinese girl in my sewing factory. We'll go twice a week. Tuesday we practice speaking and Thursday we practice reading. We'll meet more refugees at the International Centre."

"It will be nice for you to meet more Asian refugees and make more friends. And how do you like your job?" Evelyn asked.

"I don't like my boss," Lan said. "He's too friendly. He always touches me. I think I'll quit my job."

The following Friday Lan told her boss that she had found another job and would not return on Monday. Fortunately she found work in another sewing factory the next week.

When Lan went to her previous place of employment to pick up her last paycheck the boss scolded her angrily. "I'm not giving you your cheque," he said. "You lied to me and just left without giving me any notice. I would have given you a raise but now I won't give you your last cheque."

That evening Lan told Evelyn what had happened. "I know it was wrong for me to tell a lie but I just didn't want to work for him any longer. I knew that he would not let me go otherwise so I told him I had another job. I am afraid he will find out where I work now. Do you think he will tell my new boss to fire me?" Tears trickled down Lan's face.

"I'll phone him tomorrow and ask him what this is all about. I'll also phone the Labor Department to find out what the law says about this," Evelyn promised.

"I don't want to make trouble for you, Evelyn."

"That's okay, Lan. I'm sure things will work out well. Next time you want to leave a job make sure you tell your boss at least a week before you leave."

"Yes, I know that now. I'll remember."

The next day Evelyn phoned Lan's former boss. "Hello, I'm Evelyn Friesen, Lan's sponsor. She tells me that you refuse to give her her last cheque. Can you explain this to me?"

The man barked into the phone, "I thought I was helping her with a job and she walks off on me telling me she has another job! I will never hire another refugee. I've spent all this time training her and then when she's doing well she walks out on me. These people are absolutely useless to me in my factory."

"Excuse me sir," Evelyn interrupted, "but maybe you should consider the fact that she didn't know that she should have given advance n-"

Click.

"He hung up on me. One thing is sure, I would not want to work for him either and I don't blame Lan for quitting," Evelyn thought.

Evelyn phoned the Department of Law and Labor. They explained that legally Lan's boss was not obligated to pay for her last week of work because she failed to notify him in advance of her plans to leave. But her cheque would come into the department office eventually and after her case had had a hearing there was a good possibility that she would receive the cheque, especially considering that she was a recent immigrant.

Lan did get the cheque after several weeks.

Thanh started a job a number of times and then decided she didn't like it and quit. With Betty and Evelyn's help she soon found another job.

One evening she phoned Evelyn, "I've quit my job again. I'm sorry for always bothering you with my job hunting. And I don't think it is right of me to stay at jobs for such a short time. You girls always help me and let me use your names for references. But this time I will look for a job by myself. I won't use your names for references. I don't want anyone to blame you when I don't stay at the job very long."

Thanh was successful with her next job, in a restaurant, and stayed there for over a year until the restaurant closed.

After several months Nam wrote Evelyn a letter of appreciation and asked how the girls were making out. Evelyn replied, "Betty and I are having enjoyable times with the girls — helping them with their English, taking them shopping, making dental and other medical appointments for them, playing tennis, trying new recipes, playing Dutch Blitz, and inviting each other over for meals. We enjoy the girls and sometimes they even manage to teach us a few Vietnamese words. They're learning a lot and becoming fairly independent."

19

"THANK YOU GOD, FOR BRINGING MY WIFE"

The director of the refugee camp in Singapore notified Duyen that Nam's sponsors in Canada would also sponsor her. "Tomorrow you'll go for a medical check," he said, "and then if everything goes well you should be leaving in a week."

Duyen left his office with mixed feelings, "I'm not sure if this is good news or bad news," she thought. "Does Nam really want me? After all the apologies he's written I should trust him. But I feel like I hardly know him.

"We're married almost four years but we've spent so little time together. Most of the time Nam has been gone, saying that he's trying to make our future better. Will the future ever become today? Will we ever have our own place, just Nam and I? Can I dare trust that Nam is still hoping for this and working on it?"

In Stratton, Ontario, Nam had days when he felt he could hardly wait for Duyen's arrival. He longed to see her again and make her happy. On other days he wished her coming would be delayed until he had a permanent job and would be able to present her with gifts.

Nam accepted a position at the sawmill in Barwick, and boarded at Lydia and Clifford's home. At work he often thought of Duyen's arrival. "She could be coming any day. I suppose the Friesen family would expect me to show more emotion about it. I do feel excited but with all the disappointments I've experienced I've learned there's no point in getting too excited until she actually arrives. What if something goes wrong? I don't want to be disappointed again. She may be reluctant to trust me. And perhaps being with Duyen again won't be as wonderful as I've imagined."

In the evenings when he observed the warm relationship Lydia and Clifford had, Nam particularly missed Duyen's presence. "It doesn't seem right that some married couples can be together so much and others have to be separated," Nam thought. "I feel so lonely. I need Duyen. Where is she right now? How many more days will I have to wait? Are her needs taken care of or is she suffering?"

On May 28, Dad Friesen received the message that Duyen would arrive the next day. He notified Nam at work.

"Are you going to get her?" Nam asked.

"Yes. We'll be by to pick you up at three o'clock."

"I suppose I should be elated," Nam reflected as he resumed his tasks. "I won't believe that she's coming until I see her. I find my joy mixed with many worries. Where will we live? Dad told me once that married couples should live by themselves. I can't continue boarding here once Duyen arrives. I don't have money to buy a house, furniture, and appliances either. I have no means of transportation. And Duyen is bringing her younger sister along. How will I provide for all of us?"

Later, worries gave way to passion. There was light-hearted whistling and laughter from Nam at supper that evening. "I can tell Nam is getting excited about seeing Duyen, even though he can't put it into words," Lydia observed.

That night Nam could not sleep.

The next afternoon when the Friesens came to pick him up to meet Duyen in Fort Frances Nam was extremely tired and hot.

"I'm supposed to see Duyen in a few minutes," he realized as they reached Fort Frances. His heart beat faster. "I'd like to embrace her according to the Canadian custom. I'm sure that's what Mom and Dad would expect me to do. But no, I can't. Such behavior would be too strange for Duyen. In Vietnam, couples don't show physical affection in public, especially not in front of older people. I must make it as easy for Duyen as possible. I'll just greet her. We'll do our embracing later when we're alone."

Nam saw Duyen step off the bus with several other immigrants. He walked over to her and casually took her hands in his, saying, "It's so nice to see you, Duyen."

He directed Duyen to the immigration officer and assisted her and her twelve-year-old sister, Huyen, with their documents. Then he introduced her to Mom and Dad Friesen and helped her to the car.

"Aren't you cold in a short-sleeved shirt?" Duyen asked. "I find it very cold in Canada."

"No, I'm hot," Nam laughed. "Today is one of the warmer days we've had since I arrived here seven months ago."

Nam, Duyen and Huyen ate supper at Lydia's place. The travellers were exhausted so retired to bed as soon as the meal was completed.

The next morning Nam went off to work as ususal but desiring to eat his wife's cooking again, offered that Duyen would make supper. Duyen felt strange in a Canadian home where she had to use her limited English vocabulary. Communication was difficult, but together with much pointing and gesturing Lydia and Duyen managed to plan supper.

Next, Duyen went about making their bedroom look homey with the few belongings she had brought with her. On the wall she hung a picture of a young couple who were close friends of theirs. She placed a small lacey doily on their dresser.

For supper Duyen soaked pork chops and green beans in lemon. She fried the meat and vegetables and cooked the rice. She allowed herself ample time to make supper. "It's so good to have lots of water for a change," she thought. She rinsed the utensils each time she used them.

Huyen spent most of the day resting in bed; however she did take time to play with two-year old Mary Lois. Both Huyen and Duyen quickly became fond of the child, Duyen took Mary Lois in her arms. "She reminds me of Bao," she told Huyen. "Nam said she's just a few months younger than Bao. How I would love to have Bao with me. I wonder if he misses me? I hope we can have him with us soon." Duyen quickly wiped away threatening tears.

For the next night Nam, Duyen, and Huyen went to Mom and Dad Friesen's house.

Nam and Dad Friesen discussed Duyen's and Nam's future. "The school has an empty house trailer," the older man said. "The school board has decided to let you move in if you want to. The basic furniture is there so you don't need to buy anything."

"How would I get to work?" Nam wondered.

"There are a few men from this area going to work at Barwick. I'm sure we could make some kind of arrangement," Mr. Friesen assured Nam.

On Saturday the young couple moved into the school's house trailer, three kilometers from the Friesens. Then their parent-sponsors took them grocery shopping, supplying them with their basic needs. The church ladies' group showered them with blankets, pots, pans, and dishes so they were able to set up their own housekeeping right away.

On Sunday the re-united family attended church and then went to Friesens for dinner. When everyone was seated around the table ready to eat, Dad Friesen asked Nam to say the table grace.

Nam prayed, "Thank you God for bringing my wife. Help us to start a Christian home. Please take care of our son in Vietnam. Amen."

Nam continued working at the sawmill. He often got rides with Daniel Friesen, a neighbor, and once the word spread, other people offered him rides as well.

Duyen and Huyen thought it was too cold to leave the

trailer. They preferred to stay home. But sometimes they went to spend the day with Mrs. Friesen. Soon after Duyen's arrival Mom Friesen taught her how to bake white bread. It became a favorite with her. Duyen in return sewed an apron for her Canadian mother. She was eager to learn English and enlarged her vocabulary rapidly in her interaction with Mrs. Friesen.

Duyen and Huyen generally did not have much to do, however. There was no entertainment in the house, and nothing to read. They had no Vietnamese neighbors. They often chattered about their experiences in Singapore.

"You girls should have stayed in Singapore since you had so much fun there," Nam frequently teased them.

"How can you stand living here? Everything's so quiet. Doesn't the isolation bother you?" Duyen asked.

"No," he answered. "I like the quiet peacefulness. But of course I know more people by now and I don't just sit in the trailer all day."

"I've noticed that this environment has changed your character, Nam," Duyen said. "You seem more calm and relaxed than you were in Vietnam."

"Is that right? Now that you say so, maybe there's something to it. I wonder if that's why the Friesen family is so quiet and relaxed? Maybe if they lived in a big city buzzing with activity they'd be more restless."

There were always more things to learn. One day Nam attempted to make scrambled eggs. "Look what happened, Duyen. I stirred these eggs with a plastic spoon. Now my spoon disappeared among the eggs!"

Duyen's coming to Canada changed Nam's lifestyle and future plans. "I had hoped to work for a year and then go on to university. Now I have greater financial responsibilities so the question of further education will have to be dropped for a while," he concluded.

Nam and Duyen missed their son, though they were confident that all would be well with him. Duyen often cried with longing. Then Nam tried to console her. "He won't suffer," he would say. "We're going to send money to support him and there are enough people to take care of him. He's too young to worry about communism. This way you and I are freer to move about and earn money to support our relatives. My mother will give him the best possible care.

"I often wish I had taken my brother Jean with me. He's eight years old by now. I regret not having applied more pressure even though my mother wouldn't dream of parting with him then."

Duyen met the Vietnamese girls from Winnipeg when they came for Ray and Inga's wedding in early June. Duyen was delighted finally to be with other Vietnamese women. They talked for hours and begged Duyen and Huyen to join them in Winnipeg.

When Nam's job at the sawmill terminated he worried about getting another job, preferably a higher paying job.

He met a young man who advised him to try the Pulp and Paper Mill in Fort Frances. "I'm making $9.10 an hour there," he said.

"Is it hard work or hardly work?" Nam joked. "I applied there several months ago and never got a response."

"Give it another try!"

The next Friday when Phil went to Fort Frances to make meat deliveries Nam got a ride to the Pulp and Paper Mill. He felt conspicious walking into the clean office in his baggy work clothes. He recognized the secretary immediately.

"Have a seat," said the personnel manager. "What can I do for you?"

"Not much, but it could mean a lot for me." Nam sensed that this man liked his sense of humor.

He checked the files and located Nam's previous application. "Okay you were here before with a young man on crutches by the name of Ike Friesen."

"That's right," Nam said. "His family sponsored me. Ike and his brothers are loggers so I know what this business is all about."

"Do you want me to hire you?"

"Of course, yes."

"You're hired. I'll call you in a few days for orientation. You'll be on shift work."

Nam bounded off to the bank to open his first bank account in Fort Frances. Nam excitedly broke the news to Phil, "I've got the job!"

"Good for you!" congratulated Phil. "You haven't been here even a year and you'll be earning a higher wage than I am. That's not bad at all."

Towards the end of June when the call to work came Dad Friesen drove Nam to Fort Frances. "I'll find my own way back when I'm done. If nothing else, I'll take the bus back," Nam said.

At first Nam felt awkward and self-conscious at the mill. He was actually aware of the fact that he was different than the other employees. He was an Oriental, and also, although he had never taken much interest in clothing, he felt that he looked peculiar. His multi-colored shirt and short pants hung on his skinny frame.

Nam soon learned however that if he joked a lot and tried to adapt, he was fairly well accepted by his co-workers. But he found it difficult to become closely acquainted with them. "These men are different from the people I know in Stratton," Nam noted. "These guys swear a lot and try to act real 'macho,' as if they're trying to impress me."

Mentally Nam grouped the other men as 'good guys' and 'bad guys.' The good ones were interested in him and asked many questions about his background. They were impressed with Nam. Gradually he obtained a positive reputation among all the workers and even the men he had classified as bad and tough took a liking to him and gave him helpful suggestions. Nam learned to like his co-workers in spite of their different upbringings.

Nam still did not have a vehicle so decided to move in with friends in Fort Frances so he could walk to work. He tried to find a job for Duyen, but nothing was available.

Finally Duyen said, "I'll move to Winnipeg and live with

your sister and the other girls. I should easily be able to get a job there. This way we can both earn money and save towards your education. Besides, Huyen is getting restless. She would like to move to a city. What do you think about this idea, Nam?"

"Sounds all right to me," Nam agreed. "I'll be able to handle it somehow."

The church's refugee committee did not approve of their being separated again but Nam said, "If we have to be separated for a year now, but are able to have a successful life together after that, it will be worth it."

So, just a month after they arrived Mom and Dad took Duyen and Huyen to Winnipeg.

Nam stayed with friends during the month of July and then rented an apartment with Ike. As a logger, Ike put in long days. Nam worked "on call," mostly evenings and nights.

In the meantime Nam explored job possibilities for Duyen, hoping that someday soon they would be able to establish their own home.

In late fall he found a part-time job for Duyen as a cleaning lady in a motel in Fort Fances. She returned from Winnipeg and moved in with Nam and Ike. Later she took English classes in Fort Frances.

After a few months Nam and Duyen rented their own apartment and with both of them working they were able to send money to their relatives in Vietnam as well as save some for Nam's university education.

20

"IT'S WONDERFUL TO BE FREE!"

When Duyen and Huyen had moved in with the Vietnamese girls in Winnipeg at the end of June, Betty and Evelyn each took a day off from their work to go job hunting with Duyen. Duyen graciously accepted all the help she received. Her English was still very limited, but she frequently studied the two grammar books she had obtained in the refugee camp and occasionally asked Evelyn for assistance.

After a week Huyen started going to a summer school for students of English as a second language.

In July, two brothers, two sisters, and a niece of Anh and Thanh came to Canada. They all moved in with their sisters in Winnipeg as well.

As the number of tenants in the house increased the differences between them and the landlady increased also, partly due to cultural differences. In November, Mom and Dad Friesen came to settle some of the disputes. It was agreed that it would be best for everyone to find a different place to reside.

* * *

Tuan's frequent letters and phone calls to Lan eventually won her heart. She accepted his call to move to Toronto, and left Winnipeg in late November.

"Finally I have you with me again, Lan. I told you I wouldn't give up on you!" Tuan told her when he met her at the airport.

Lan returned his welcome with one of her shy smiles.

"I've rented a room for you in the apartment building where my roommate and I live," Tuan explained. "I have also made arrangements for you to work in the cafeteria in the University of Toronto where I study. Later on, if you want, you may also attend school. I'm so glad you decided to come to Toronto, and I want you to be happy."

"Thank you for all you've done for me, Tuan. Right now I feel strange and scared. This is such a big city." Lan pulled her coat tightly around her shivering body. "What if I won't be what Tuan expects me to be?" she worried.

Tuan made sure Lan was well taken care of and applied much effort to make her feel secure and confident. They spent many hours discussing their experiences as recent immigrants to Canada.

"I've never doubted my decision to escape my country to find freedom," Tuan reflected one day. "The idea was born more than two years before I escaped, soon after South Vietnam collapsed. My parents tried desperately to get the family out of the country. We didn't know where we would go. I thought I'd be happy ending up anywhere, any non-communist neighboring country. But failure followed failure, and as time went on my determination grew. It was solidified by compulsory political meetings, by revolutionary songs blasting into my ears everyday from every corner of the streets, and by the sight of broken families, the poor, the hungry, and the oppressed.

"I still remember one day, in the morning, a dozen policemen climbed over the gate of my house to tell us to get out the next day. In the afternoon at school I was told to write an essay about the Premier's great ideals and contribution to the country in an exam. I bit part of my pen into pieces and could put down only a few lines. Of course I failed the exam.

"We attempted to flee but all ended up in jail. All of us

were freed after three months, expect my father. Four months later I planned a successful escape with the help of Nam and Li. Unfortunately the responsibility and stress on me at the time was too much and I failed to bring any of my five brothers with me."

"I know how you feel. I had to leave my sisters and I don't know if I'll ever see them again," Lan reminded him.

"What would you say has been the greatest difficulty for the Asian refugees who immigrated to Canada?" Lan continued after a pause.

"For the Vietnamese in Canada, learning English is probably the greatest difficulty in adapting to a new life. For most of us adults this will remain a problem for the rest of our lives. Also, many people lose the social position they once had. They have to take any job to survive. But I think it's something most refugees can cope with. They're happy and have much hope in their children. For younger people Canada is still a land of opportunity. This second-largest country in the world, with only 25 million people and a lot of natural resources can grow and prosper if we work together. I think the current recession is only temporary."

"So do you feel like you're at home in Canada now, Tuan?"

"In this diverse society," Tuan replied, "people's attitudes towards each other and the way people treat one another, even though less than perfect, is something I admire. I will never forget how I was received here. The compassion of the Canadian people has helped me in accepting this land as my country."

* * *

The rest of the Winnipeg household moved into a more spacious house in the beginning of December, 1980. Here they had more privacy and liberty to entertain their friends according to their customs.

Through work and school they quickly made many friends. Two of the most popular guests were Thu and Duc who came to Canada as government-sponsored refugees.

These fellows offered to take the girls to work in the mornings and took them shopping on Saturdays. The girls gladly accepted these offers because they disliked being dependent on the transit buses. In return for the rides they often invited Thu and Duc over for meals.

Although they did not know each other from Vietnam, Thu and Anh discovered that their parents lived fairly close together in Saigon. Anh loved singing while Thu played guitar so they frequently sang at school and other social events. As they became fonder of each other they contacted their parents about getting married. The parents then met and became acquainted. They decided the marriage would please them. Anh and Thu celebrated their marriage on August 1, 1981.

Duc sought Thanh's love and asked her to marry him. Thanh reasoned, "I want to be a positive contribution to society and feel I can do this better by getting married." She consented to Duc's request. Their marriage followed a month after Anh and Thu's, on September 6.

* * *

In the beginning of September, 1981 Nam and Duyen moved to Winnipeg so that Nam could attend the University of Manitoba. He enrolled in a computer program and Duyen went back to work in the sewing factory where she had worked previously. "I'm glad I'm able to skimp and save enough to buy clothing for Bao and send it to Vietnam," Duyen told Nam. "I'm so anticipating the time when we'll have him with us in Canada."

Phuong and Huyen lived with Nam and Duyen. Phuong worked in a sewing factory and Huyen attended school.

On July 30, 1983 Phuong married Lam, a brother to Anh and Thanh. A year later Huyen married.

"Now we have the apartment to ourselves, Duyen, just like we've dreamed about for so many years," Nam said to Duyen as Huyen moved out with the last of her belongings. "How will you enjoy that?

"Oh, I'll love it," Duyen said, "except for one thing. I wish Bao could be with us." Duyen's eyes grew misty. "Do you miss him, Nam?"

"Yes, I do. I don't think about him during the day when I'm at university but I sure think about him when I see other couples with children. Remember Monday night when our neighbors were here?"

"Yes, I remember. You sure enjoyed playing with their kids. Their oldest son is six, just a few days older than Bao is now. When you romped around with those three, I couldn't help wondering what it would be like to see you play with our Bao."

"Me too. We've come a long way in our fight for freedom but we're still not finished. Just one more year and I'll be finished with my university studies. As soon as I get a decent job we'll be able to save money to sponsor my family and Bao."

"Isn't it already over a year ago since we applied to sponsor them?"

"Yes, but it takes time. Gaining freedom is neither quick nor cheap. But with time, money, and determination as our tools we'll continue fighting until we've gained freedom for the rest of our family."

"Sometimes I feel I can't wait any longer," Duyen said, beginning to cry. "My thoughts go to Bao every night and I long to hold him in my arms again."

"But when you look back to our life in Vietnam and compare it with what we have now, don't you agree it's been worth the suffering?" Nam asked.

"Yes. Yes definitely," Duyen answered, wiping her eyes. "Here we have the freedom to get jobs, to study, to make our own choices. . . ."

They sat in silence for several minutes, reflecting on the past and the present.

"Sometimes it all seems so far away, so long ago," Nam mused. "My feelings about communist control in Vietnam haven't changed but I've learned that I can't do anything about the situation. The war was a mistake on the part of the Americans, I think. They simply underestimated the Vietnamese. The war proved again that fighting solves no problems. Hopefully we'll all learn from the mistakes of the past.

"You know, I often dream of returning. If the political situation changed, I would. Maybe if I'd been born into a communist society my life would have been easier, but trying to adjust to communist control after being used to a different political system was just too much of a change. I just couldn't live without freedom.

"In some ways though, we continue to pay for freedom." Nam went on thoughtfully. "There are pitfalls. For one thing, it's difficult for Asian refugees to develop intimate personal relationships with Canadians. Canadians seem very materialistic. They don't seem to need people. For me as a student this isn't a problem because I'm usually busy studying, but whenever I watch a movie I'd rather be with you or a friend than by myself."

"This could be a difficulty for your parents when they come here," Duyen pointed out.

"I've often thought of that," Nam admitted. "But by the time they get here I'll be finished with university. Hopefully I'll be able to spend a lot of time with them. At any rate, they'll have each other and the rest of my family."

Duyen replied, "I often hear of older people who came to Canada and later regret it. They find learning a new language too difficult. Their children are all away at work or school and suddenly they find themselves very much alone, with no one to live for."

"It's even harder for government-sponsored refugees," Nam stated. "It's a proven fact that privately-sponsored refugees get established more quickly. They automatically have more connections. Take our case for example. We had little difficulty finding jobs because we could use Canadians as references."

"Speaking of pitfalls, isn't it funny how strangers judge us to be uncivilized and stupid when we can't communicate in English?" Duyen remarked.

"That's for sure," Nam agreed. "Most Canadians seem

generally uninformed as to who we are. They stereotype us and expect us to be ignorant of modern technology because we don't know their language and had to flee our home country. If more Canadians cared to get to know us as individuals they would change their opinion of us, I'm sure. We have much to contribute to society if given a fair chance."

"Many of us are made to feel inferior because we're Orientals," Duyen stated. "I think of all the young people who so badly need guidance. Their parents are too old to learn English quickly and help their children, and they soon lose control in this society where children aren't taught to respect their elders. These kids often turn out to cause disturbances on the streets. When they get into trouble others taunt them about being ignorant 'boat people,' provoking them to fight, and then our people are accused of being the guilty ones."

"I see another pitfall for our people," Nam said. "Many Vietnamese people are struggling hard to make a living. They lack the language, specific skills, money, and friends needed in order to progress. Again, this is more difficult for government-sponsored refugees. In their desperation they throw away anything related to the Vietnamese culture. When I left Vietnam I resolved to leave the language too but now it bothers me to see how many of our people refuse to speak Vietnamese to their Canadian born children. The English they use is far from correct. Why don't they transmit the Vietnamese culture and let someone who will teach English correctly handle that language? Once the children are grown I think the parents will regret their negligence in this area. Our children should be taught to be proud of their heritage. We should be proud of what we are and have, because that's how God made us. In fact, this country consists largely of one-time immigrants contributing their assets and working together. Our dear parents, the Friesens, were once immigrants too."

"In spite of the disadvantages, do you feel that you've gained the freedom you sought for so many years?" Duyen asked.

"Yes, I do," Nam answered. "It's wonderful to be free to work and study and sleep whenever and wherever I choose." He laughed. "People may think I have weird tastes but then I say, 'So what? It's a free country!'

"Yes, Duyen," Nam continued seriously," I'm truly thankful to God for the numerous freedoms I'm able to enjoy here. My biggest desire now is to obtain this same freedom for our son Bao and the rest of my family. What we have now must be shared."